PILGRIM JOURNEYS

The Bible Reading Fellowship
15 The Chambers, Vineyard
Abingdon OX14 3FE
brf.org.uk

The Bible Reading Fellowship (BRF) is a Registered Charity (233280)

ISBN 978 0 85746 513 9
All rights reserved
First published 2017
10 9 8 7 6 5 4 3 2 1 0

Text © Sally Welch 2017
This edition © The Bible Reading Fellowship 2017
Front cover images: (top) Bell Harry Tower fan vaulting, Canterbury Cathedral, Kent, photo © Terence Waeland / Alamy; (below) St Swithun's Way, photo © Jim Ringland. Back cover image © Thinkstock

The author asserts the moral right to be identified as the author of this work

Acknowledgements
Scripture quotations from The New Revised Standard Version of the Bible, Anglicised edition, copyright © 1989, 1995 by the Division of Christian Education of the National Council of the Churches of Christ in the United States of America. Used by permission. All rights reserved.

Every effort has been made to trace and contact copyright owners for material used in this resource. We apologise for any inadvertent omissions or errors, and would ask those concerned to contact us so that full acknowledgement can be made in the future.

A catalogue record for this book is available from the British Library

Printed and bound by CPI Group (UK) Ltd, Croydon CR0 4YY

SALLY WELCH

PILGRIM JOURNEYS

Pilgrimage for walkers and armchair travellers

Contents

Introduction

The path stretches out ahead, sunk deep between the hedgerows, which rise to a height of some six or eight feet either side, like green walls, festooned with flowers and plants as if celebrating some perpetual festival. Two rows of oak trees tower over the thick hedges, stern and tall, their solid trunks reaching high into the sky, branches intertwining across and over, creating a tunnel-like space, cool and green. The light is dim, filtered by thousands of green leaves carefully positioned so that each one should catch some life-giving light. Here and there, a gap in the branches allows a narrow shaft of sunlight to pierce the shade, illuminating a stone or a plant like a spotlight on the carving of an ancient and historic building. Narrow and edged with grass, the honey-coloured stones and mud show evidence of the hundreds of feet that have passed that way, pilgrims following the Way—seeking transformation, enlightenment, peace, God—all sorts of names have been given over the centuries. It is inviting and exciting, beckoning us on to discovery and adventure, encounter and delight; we need simply to take that first step.

Such paths can be found all over the British Isles and Europe, leading through wild countryside and large cities to pilgrimage destinations as famous as Rome or as little-known as Binsey. Pilgrimage destinations such as Iona and Lindisfarne within the UK receive over 150,000 visitors a year, while Santiago de Compostela in Spain numbers its pilgrims in the millions.

However, such bald statistics do not do justice to the growing interest in the spirituality of pilgrimage as something not simply concerned with the journeys of those physically travelling but as a way of living and thinking. True pilgrims do not cease to be pilgrims once the journey is complete: they take the lessons and insights learned from the journey back into their lives at home. These lessons are often learned through encountering and overcoming the challenges and difficulties of the journey, however long or short it is. They are reinforced by the hours of reflection that are part of the gift of a pilgrimage—time and space to think and reflect, to allow insights to sink deep into heart and mind. On the return to everyday life, with its daily routines and obligations, it is easy to forget those lessons, to bury them deep beneath the usual round of work and recreation. How valuable might they be if they were incorporated instead into a pattern of praying and living that could gradually conform the life of the pilgrim to one of constant pilgrimage, sharing the route with others who sought the way of the gospel, looking towards the eternal destination, the heavenly city which is our goal.

This book aims to share some of the lessons learnt by pilgrims while on their journeys, and to show how such lessons do not stop at the end of the journey but can be adopted and absorbed by those who have travelled and those who have not. Insights gained on the journey can be incorporated into the spiritual life of every day, bringing new ways of relationship with God and with our fellow Christians, offering support and encouragement as we face the joys and challenges of life. Using pilgrim routes as a starting point, each chapter explores a different aspect of pilgrimage, offering reflections and approaches that can be used at home and away.

A brief history of pilgrimage

The idea of pilgrimage—a spiritual journey to a sacred place—is buried deep within our understanding of spirituality and religious practice. Ever since those first disciples rushed to see for themselves the place where Jesus had been buried and was now no longer present, men and women have travelled to sites made significant either by the deeds carried out or words spoken there or by the fact that a holy man or woman lived or was buried there.

The practice of making a special journey to a place where significant spiritual events have occurred, along a route made holy in itself by the numberless thousands who have made the journey before, and, on arrival at the site, of connecting somehow with the events that took place there, has had a huge influence not only on the spiritual history of the British Isles but also on the physical infrastructure. Routes were laid down by the feet of the faithful travellers, glorious buildings made possible by the donations of those who visited places where relics lay in state, and a network of abbeys built to support the needs of those travellers.

For many hundreds of years, even during times when injunctions were made by religious leaders against the practice, men and women hoping for healing, revelation or spiritual insight have travelled to places where, it is felt, the gap between heaven and earth is smaller, where the actions of saints may break into the lives of ordinary people, transforming them. Recent years have seen a dramatic revival in an appreciation of its benefits, some of which find their roots in an awareness of the long history of similar walkers, a feeling of walking in the path of those who have gone before over the years, both well-known and ordinary members of the 'community of saints'.

The reasons behind Jewish and Christian pilgrimage lie in the Bible. A theme that runs throughout the Old Testament in particular is that of a wandering nation. Abraham was the founding father of Islam, Judaism and Christianity, and it is to him that the first imperative to go is given: 'Go from your country and your kindred and your father's house to the land that I will show you. I will make of you a great nation, and I will bless you, and make your name great, so that you will be a blessing' (Genesis 12:1–2). Abraham lived as a nomad, and the tradition was continued by Moses, who led his people through the wilderness for 40 years after their escape from slavery in Egypt.

God himself preferred not to have a settled base, as his words revealed when David proposed building a temple in Jerusalem (2 Samuel 7:5–6). Later, however, a temple was built by Solomon, which stood from around 1000BC until about 587, when it was destroyed and the Jews were eventually banished from the city. A second temple, built in around 538BC, lasted until its destruction by the Romans in 63BC, and it was this second temple that saw the flourishing of pilgrimage to Jerusalem as the two feasts of Passover and Sukkot reminded all Jewish people of their wandering history.

Although there is less overt mention of pilgrimage in the New Testament, nevertheless there is evidence that Jesus obeyed the call to go to Jerusalem at festival times. The records of his life in the Gospels depict him as frequently on the move: 'Foxes have holes, and birds of the air have nests; but the Son of Man has nowhere to lay his head' (Luke 9:58). After the resurrection, the disciples continued to travel, journeying throughout the known world as they spread the story of Christ.

With these imperatives in mind, and with a natural curiosity and desire to see the sites where the key episodes of Christ's life took place, it would not be surprising to discover that Christian pilgrimage began almost as soon as the empty tomb was discovered. However, the terrible persecution of those early followers of Christ would have done much to prevent a formal system of travel to the holy places from developing.

Such journeys may have become easier with Emperor Constantine's declaration that Christianity was to become the formal religion of Rome. Helena, the mother of the emperor, journeyed to Jerusalem and other holy sites in AD326, bringing back to Europe many souvenirs of her visit in the shape of nails from the crucifixion, pieces of the true cross and other relics. It may have been Helena who encouraged Constantine to build basilicas at the places where Jesus' birth and burial occurred. Certainly this paved the way for other Christians to visit the sites mentioned in both the Old and the New Testaments, and there is evidence that they did so. Even in 325, pilgrim guides were beginning to appear, as the nun Egeria described her experiences of travelling through the Holy Land, sharing with those who were unable to make the journey themselves something of the nature of these places.

Constantine also developed other Christian sites, such as the Lateran Church in Rome to house the tomb of St Peter, and pilgrimage became an accepted way for people to demonstrate their religious intentions. But it was not only the major sites that became ever more popular as a way of expressing devotion to the saints. Gradually a body of history developed on the lives and actions of local saints, missionaries to the shores of Britain who sought to carry the news of the gospel to this hostile land. These missionaries left behind those whom they had converted, who followed in their footsteps, demonstrating the love of God in words and actions. The places where miracles and revelations occurred—healings, conversions, miraculous events—became, in their turn, sacred, although on a more domestic scale. Those who could not afford the time or money to make the lengthy and dangerous trips to the pilgrimage sites of Europe and the Middle East could find, in a shorter, more local journey, something of the experience and benefits of such a trip. Each pilgrimage, however short, afforded an insight into the spirituality of the journey.

In time, the sites associated with the Celtic saints of the seventh and eighth centuries—Iona, Crouagh Patrick, Lindisfarne—became places of pilgrimage themselves, as men and women sought contact with the great names of Celtic Christianity. These sites and others around

England became more popular as travelling to the Holy Land became more problematic. The final fall of Jerusalem in 1453 meant that European sites such as Rome and Santiago de Compostela in Spain became the main goal of those wishing to make a lengthy pilgrimage. Santiago housed the remains of St James, reportedly discovered In 835. Pilgrims began visiting this shrine from the tenth century, the first recorded English pilgrims arrived in the late eleventh century and, by the twelfth century, the pilgrimage was highly organised. Routes from all over Europe converged on a single route through Spain, supported by an infrastructure of hostels, guest houses and large churches for devotions along the route, often themselves housing shrines and relics and becoming pilgrimage destinations in their own right.

Within England itself, shrines were also founded around the country's major saints. Walsingham, the site where, in 1061, the noblewoman Richildis received a vision telling her to build a replica of the house of the nativity, rapidly became popular, aided by the establishment of an Augustinian priory there in 1153 and visits from several monarchs. The shrine of Thomas Becket, Archbishop of Canterbury, murdered by Henry II in 1170, rapidly became a site of pilgrimage, with even Henry II himself bowing to the inevitable and making a penitential journey there.

These shrines, along with lesser home-grown saints such as Swithun at Winchester and Oswald at Worcester, became very popular. As pilgrimage became part of English religious practice, the country was crossed and recrossed with pilgrimage routes, encouraging trade and a growing range of businesses dedicated to the needs of pilgrims. During the 'golden years' of pilgrimage—from the early eleventh to the early 16th century—up to one-fifth of the population of Europe is estimated to have had connections with pilgrimage, either as pilgrims themselves or maintaining its infrastructure. Elaborate tables of penance were drawn up during the 14th century to illustrate which sites promised most time off from purgatory for each particular offence committed. The *Liber Sancti Jacobi*, a twelfth-century manual for pilgrims to Santiago de Compostela, gave route directions, liturgies and a reminder that a pilgrimage was not simply an excursion but a serious penitential undertaking. Clearly, even by then, there were concerns that such journeys were not always undertaken in the correct spirit.

The seeds of decline were fertilised by the growing danger of travel through not only the Middle East but Europe itself, stricken with conflicts both internal and international, and they came to fruition with the Reformation in the 16th century, when both the church and the state worked to suppress the phenomenon of pilgrimage.

Despite the vast numbers of people who undertook pilgrimage, however, there had always been some resistance to the idea. From as early as the fourth century, writers such as Jerome and Gregory of Nyssa questioned its necessity, believing that God could be found everywhere, not just in holy places. There was a danger in taking the focus of the soul away from spiritual progress to concentrate on the merely physical journey. These concerns were combined with a growing awareness that a journey away from a person's home might allow them the sort of sexual and moral freedoms that were corrupting and irreligious. Those who made large amounts of money from offering hospitality to pilgrims at vastly inflated rates, taking advantage of their lack of local knowledge and customs, also came under criticism. Thomas à Kempis commented that pilgrimage rarely brought the pilgrim spiritually closer to God.

By the time of the Reformation, opposition to pilgrimage had increased. It was better to spend the money on the poor than on travel, it was argued, especially when opportunities for misbehaviour were so plentiful. Curiosity about the material world was seen as preventing concentration on the world to come: the interior journey was thought to be the best pilgrimage. As Luther wrote, 'Rather than walk about holy places we can thus pause at our own thoughts, examine our hearts and visit the real promised land and paradise of eternal life.' Also, the pilgrim destinations, where the body parts of dead saints were knelt by and prayed at, were beginning to be seen as idolatrous. Although the destruction of shrines and the dissolution of the monasteries by

Henry VIII has been traditionally viewed as heralding the end of the heyday of pilgrimage, perhaps more responsible was the gradual change in mindset experienced during this period.

In the feudalism of the Middle Ages, the bond constituted by the relationship between the lord and the peasant, whereby protection was offered in return for service, was mirrored in the bond between saint and worshipper. The individualism of the Reformation brought a drop in devotion to saints by those who felt that they were freed from 'middle men'. Christians accepted the grace of God as a free gift, without the ties of mutual obligation.

In 1536, the Bishop of St David's ordered pilgrimage to that shrine to cease and relics to be removed, and Becket's shrine in Canterbury Cathedral was also destroyed. Gradually, during the 16th century, most of the shrines throughout Protestant Britain and Europe were destroyed, with a corresponding growth of emphasis on the internal or spiritual pilgrimage, the inner journey of faith. John Bunyan's *Pilgrim's Progress* summed up this metaphor of life itself as a journey to the eternal city of Jerusalem, and the sentiment was echoed by churchmen and officials.

The rise of the Romantic and Neo-Gothic movements brought pilgrimage once again into the realms of acceptable practice. The 19th century saw a resurgence of interest in the Holy Land and Rome, encouraged by companies such as Cook's Tours, who provided tours to both places. The appearance of the Virgin Mary to a 14-year-old girl at Lourdes in 1858 gave rise to a new site, dedicated to healing, with other sites, including Fatima, Iona, Taizé and Medugorje, gaining credence in the 20th century.

The numbers of people undertaking pilgrimages both within the UK and further afield are now growing year by year. Other sites within the UK are developing opportunities for pilgrimage: the people involved in running cathedrals are exploring ways of turning tourists, interested in the historical facts and architectural triumphs of their buildings, into pilgrims who might become open to the peace and beauty of the cathedral, offering an opportunity to reflect and pray. Dioceses such as Oxford and East Anglia are working to develop networks of pilgrim paths around their areas, the Thames Pilgrim Way being just one initiative. Smaller churches too are adapting their buildings to provide hospitality to walkers and pilgrims who pause in their journey to offer prayers for themselves and others. An awareness of the possibilities of pilgrimage is becoming a significant part of Christian spirituality once more, bringing with it opportunities even for those for whom a journey to distant lands is not a possibility.

The Routes

1   Be true to your journey

ST COLUMBA'S WAY (Iona to St Andrews)

Do not be ashamed, then, of the testimony about our Lord or of me his prisoner, but join with me in suffering for the gospel, relying on the power of God, who saved us and called us with a holy calling, not according to our works but according to his own purpose and grace. This grace was given to us in Christ Jesus before the ages began, but it has now been revealed through the appearing of our Saviour Christ Jesus, who abolished death and brought life and immortality to light through the gospel. For this gospel I was appointed a herald and an apostle and a teacher, and for this reason I suffer as I do. But I am not ashamed, for I know the one in whom I have put my trust, and I am sure that he is able to guard until that day what I have entrusted to him. Hold to the standard of sound teaching that you have heard from me, in the faith and love that are in Christ Jesus. Guard the good treasure entrusted to you, with the help of the Holy Spirit living in us.

2 TIMOTHY 1:8–14

Unless you live in the west of Scotland, the journey to Iona is lengthy, time-consuming and, however economical you are, expensive. To begin with, you have to find your way to a mainline airport or bus or train station. This is, in itself, often problematic and may well involve different types of transport—local bus or car, branch train line—before the large terminus is reached that will provide you with transport to Glasgow. From there you can hire a car or take a smaller, slower bus or train to the west coast town of Oban. This will inevitably involve a period of waiting, for only the luckiest can get connections all in a row, like dominoes waiting to fall into place.

Often, the best part of the day has been taken up by the time Oban is reached, so a bed must be found for the night or a tent pitched in a local campsite. It doesn't matter if you don't sleep well, for you will have to be up early in order to make your way to the ferry port to catch the small passenger ferry which will take you, providing the weather permits, across the estuary to the Isle of Mull. A journey across Mull ends with another ferry crossing, to arrive finally on the tiny island of Iona. By this time you may well be feeling that you have journeyed enough and have still only just reached your starting point! But the numinous quality of Iona, the island so precariously perched at the edge of Scotland's rugged coastline, prey to the battering of Atlantic storms and grown hardy and rugged as a consequence, will prove an ample reward for your efforts.

Although every pilgrim is anxious to begin the journey as soon as possible, it is worth spending a few days on this holy island, soaking yourself in the prayerful peace of the place, taking part in the services at the abbey, rejoicing in the wildness of the landscape and the generosity of the inhabitants towards the thousands of visitors who arrive each year seeking the space and peace that this remote place has to offer. The main purpose of the journey must not be ignored, however: pausing to ask God's blessing on themselves, pilgrims must then retrace their steps to the mainland, there to step out on the 200 miles or so that will take them right across Scotland, from west coast to east. The arrival point will be the enchanting city of St Andrews, famous not only for its university but for its royal connections.

As is to be expected, St Columba's Way is challenging and hard work. The path is rugged, the terrain is often difficult, and route-finding isn't always easy. The pilgrimage is made harder by the unpredictable weather, storms of rain being a real possibility, whatever month you travel in, compounded by the clouds of midges that swarm around you from May onwards, said to be the fiercest in the world. A foolproof deterrent has yet to be found, although many different repellents have their fans, who use many lines of type to praise them on web forums devoted especially to the subject.

The rewards are enormous, however—breathtaking views of the Scottish countryside, green meadows running alongside clear sparkling rivers, amazing vistas of rolling hills, and interesting towns to explore. Above all, there is a sense of community with those first brave individuals who set off, armed with no more than a deep knowledge of their calling, to bring the news of Christ's love to the fierce warlike tribes of the hills.

To the Irish saint Columba is attributed the founding of the monastery on the isolated island of Iona. Originally from Donegal, Columba was ordained priest before the age of 25 and was instrumental in establishing monasteries in Derry, Durrow and Kells. However, legend has it that a family feud, in which Columba played a significant part, resulted in a tremendous battle between his clan and that of the Irish overlord, Diarmuid. Over 3000 were killed in the course of the battle. Columba was held, by himself and others, as morally responsible for their deaths, so he resolved to travel overseas and claim as many souls for Christ as he had allowed to perish unshriven. Accordingly, he and twelve fellow monks set out in their small, frail coracles across the Irish Sea, landing on the island of Iona in 563. There he built a monastery which was to remain his home for the rest of his life, becoming famed as a centre of learning and a missionary stronghold.

It is rather a sad fact that, for most members of churches, a sense of calling is seen mostly in terms of a call to ordination. Beginning with an interior longing, an often vague and certainly difficult-to-articulate sense of being drawn to a different role within the church community, the calling is often validated by members of the community itself. Men and women, when speaking of the journey that has brought them to priesthood, tell of friends and fellow church attenders asking them why they were not seeking ordination or, more astonishingly, assuming simply that they already were. This call is then tested by the leaders of a church organisation and the aspiring priest is given various tasks to do—books to read; projects to undertake, perhaps; and essays to write on their spiritual formation and why they feel called to be a priest, how they understand the priesthood and what their future intentions are. Finally, appearing before an assessment panel of some kind, those whose calling is validated by the church are accepted for more training and formation before that heady day, often many years since the first hesitant response to what was believed to be a call from God, when they are ordained deacon or priest.

But to confine the definition of a Christian calling simply to this narrow path is to miss being part of the joyous community of Christian men and women who have been challenged, throughout the centuries, to conform their lives to God to carry out his will and fulfil his purpose for them in a range of tasks and roles—as varied as they are demanding, and as diverse as they are essential for the job of bringing near the kingdom. The call is not for all of us to become members of the priesthood, for then the danger would be that we gather together in a small self-serving community and never look beyond the boundaries of that one task for signs of glory. The call is not simply for a few chosen ones to become the elite, the leaders, the only ones who matter. The call goes out among all God's children to live their lives in a way that enables them to reach their full potential as people of God, loving, caring, active in the work of the kingdom, reflective in their relationship with God, and sharing Christ's saving work on earth.

I have never doubted that I was called to become a pilgrim—called by God to pray as I journeyed on foot, facing the challenges of the route with a growing confidence and courage, learning from the people I met along the way, sharing their burdens physically as well as spiritually, bringing back to my community the insights and lessons I have gained in order to weave them into my life and theirs. If a period of time passes when I have not undertaken a pilgrimage, I become restless and ill at ease. I am aware that I am being called to something, some task which I cannot discern but which I must carry out. Only when I make the connection between the restlessness and the length of time since I last undertook a spiritual journey, and begin to plan the next one, can I find peace.

Admittedly, this restlessness could merely be physical and spiritual boredom; I could have mistaken a dissatisfaction with my current way of life and my longing for adventure for a genuine call from God to take up my backpack and set off into the unknown, there to challenge my soul and body to greater fitness for God's purposes for me. Perhaps. But the cost in time, effort and financial outlay would make that seem unlikely. Maybe the greater sin is to ascribe the whisper of God's voice to join him on the road simply to human ennui, and hence to do nothing about it. So we may ignore the faint whisper that we hear, no more than a breath, telling us that we should be focusing our hearts and minds on a certain aspect of our lives, growing it and developing it in the name of the kingdom.

We may feel that the task we are being gently nudged into undertaking, this role that we are unwilling to assume, is too great for us—the challenges too overwhelming, the objective too difficult to obtain. But to put aside the call of God because we are afraid is to ignore the response he has made to countless others who have put forward that defence for their reaction. Thus did Moses when he was called by God to save the children of Israel, to lead them out of slavery in Egypt to the freedom of the promised land.

Even when asked by God himself, even when standing barefoot on holy ground, in awe at God's presence, Moses is filled with fear at the task he is being asked to undertake, and puts forward all sorts of objections: no one will believe him; everyone knows he is a sinner; he won't be able to make them do what he says (Exodus 3:11—4:10). God breathes his reassurance upon the fearful Moses: 'Say to the Israelites, "I AM has sent me to you",' he answers, promising his presence and his power (Exodus 3:14).

Jonah, too, runs away when challenged by God to make the people of Nineveh face up to their wrong behaviour. But however far Jonah runs, God finds him; and however many excuses we make for our own inaction, God will find us! How can we grow except by taking the steps necessary to fulfil God's purpose in us? How will the kingdom grow unless we, God's hands and feet here on earth, devote ourselves to the task?

On the other hand, it might be that the things we are being asked to do in the name of Christ seem too trivial for us to undertake. Perhaps we dream of carrying the gospel into the darkest places of the world, or simply into the hidden and forlorn places of our local community, but find ourselves constantly prevented from doing so by irritating minor tasks of administration or the constant demands upon our time and resources made by the people who are dependent upon us. Maybe we dream of the time when we can be finally released from these burdens of caring, of trivial detail, into the open spaces of truly challenging gospel tasks.

Here again, however, if we pause to reflect, if we put down our dreams of greatness—even greatness in God's name—we find that it is in the detail, the trivia, that God is to be found. Swept along by the urgency of Jairus' need to find healing for his daughter, who is sick to the point of death, Jesus stops mid-stride. 'Who touched my clothes?' he asks the crowd, and it is not until the woman with the constant haemorrhage comes forward and is healed that Jesus continues on his way (Mark 5:24–34). 'Let the little children come to me,' he says when the disciples try to drive away these small annoyances and their plaguing mothers (Luke 18:15–16). Don't ignore the seemingly inconsequential, for these are the building blocks of the kingdom.

Some of our family pilgrimages, made when the children were small and unpredictable, could not have been carried out if we had travelled independently. Small babies tire easily, even when they are set high on a person's back, with a good view of the countryside and an endless supply of biscuits. Older children, too, may become bored or fatigued by walking through the industrial outskirts of a major town, or it may become too much of a task to be constantly dodging heavy lorries as they rumble past. Although we carried all our daily luggage on our backs, to set off without emergency supplies of nappies and at least some baby food would have been irresponsible. So my parents would gallantly offer to accompany each journey, driving the heavier inessentials to and from each stopping place, meeting us at lunch time with cups of tea brewed on their ancient primus stove, occasionally sweeping up a weary grandchild to spend the afternoon in the hotel swimming pool. (They did not feel the need to share pilgrim accommodation.) Without them, we could not have undertaken these journeys, and the experiences of the road would have been lost to us.

To begin with, my parents refused to acknowledge their status as fellow pilgrims, considering that driving at speed through country lanes on the way to spy out a suitable picnic place was not truly pilgrim-worthy. Then one day my father met us in the company of an elderly woman, very dignified and gracious. He had stopped her in her slow walk to the nearby bread shop and asked if she had seen us, evidently describing us in his usual picturesque language, for she was at first quite startled, it seemed. Then, when my father added the fact that we were on pilgrimage, she relaxed: evidently pilgrims were the acceptable side of eccentric. 'And you,' she said, turning to my father, 'you are a pilgrim also?' He hastily denied it, responding that, as grandparents, they were merely the back-up team. The lady responded, 'No, no. True pilgrimage happens in the heart.' Then she placed her hand on my father's chest, almost in blessing: 'You have the heart of a pilgrim.'

Everyday, nondescript tasks; small gestures of loving kindness; a place on the coffee rota, a visit to a lonely person, a willingness to tidy up after the Sunday school children have swept like a hurricane through the church building—all these call us to the role of servant, to follow in Christ's footsteps by humbly hitching up our garments, tying an apron round our waist and kneeling to wash the feet of our fellow Christians in whatever way is asked of us.

Reflection

Listening to God's call for us and being open to what he is asking us to do is a challenging and frightening task to undertake. It may be that we will find ourselves called to a task that we feel is beyond us or beneath us. Perhaps we are being asked to change the way we live our life or carry out our job, or even to change our job. However, it is only by listening that we will hear, and only by hearing that we will be able to undertake, and only by undertaking the task or role that God has given to us that we will find our true selves, and peace.

For this reflection you will need nothing more than some empty sheets of paper, a pencil or pen and some crayons. The larger the paper, the better: you can use scissors to cut it smaller if you find you need to do so. Use pencil crayons or felt-tipped pens—whatever you can find, that suits you best. Set aside a large amount of time—at least two hours. You may find you can complete the reflection in less time than this, but knowing that you have more than enough time will help you to relax and focus more fully.

Now simply write or draw your spiritual journey—the story of your relationship with God and how it has brought you to the place where you are today. You may wish to draw it in the shape of a long pilgrim path, travelling up the page, with illustrations along the way for significant events. You might include a picture of the church where you were baptised, for example, or the face of someone important to your spiritual development. You may wish to draw using the technique of a graph, with high points and low points, writing down what the highs and lows were and why they had such a positive or negative impact on your life. You don't need to be chronological at all: some incidents that happen in earlier years reveal their truths only later in life. To illustrate this, you can cut your paper into pieces and draw or write a different episode or incident on each piece. When you have filled in all the pieces, put them together like a patchwork quilt—the fabric of your life.

When you have filled in as much as you can remember, put the paper to one side and leave it for a while. You can leave it for some hours or even days, or perhaps you will feel you need longer to reflect. Keep the paper in your mind, however, and allow it to come to the surface in your quiet times or reflective moments, when travelling to work or tidying up, as well as when praying and reflecting. Allow God to speak to you about your life, and see if any patterns emerge.

When you feel ready and have enough time set aside to make you feel comfortable, look again at what you have drawn or written. Can you see God's hand at work in your life? What patterns are there? Can you see times when you have ignored or evaded God's call? How did this feel? Ask God to guide you towards the right path, to make clear to you the direction in which you must walk so that you can carry out his will.

2 Carry only what is necessary

A certain ruler asked him, 'Good Teacher, what must I do to inherit eternal life?' Jesus said to him, 'Why do you call me good? No one is good but God alone. You know the commandments: "You shall not commit adultery; You shall not murder; You shall not steal; You shall not bear false witness; Honour your father and mother."' He replied, 'I have kept all these since my youth.' When Jesus heard this, he said to him, 'There is still one thing lacking. Sell all that you own and distribute the money to the poor, and you will have treasure in heaven; then come, follow me.' But when he heard this, he became sad; for he was very rich.
LUKE 18:18–23

My daughter and I had stopped on the Via Ingles, perhaps, too long. We had taken the time to light the stove and make a proper cup of tea rather than simply taking swigs from our water bottles as we walked along. The tea was refreshing and we were enjoying the satisfaction that comes from a day's journey almost complete and the security of a hotel room booked in advance—a rare luxury, which meant that we did not have to hurry to secure a precious place in the hostel. The heat of the day had lessened and we had enjoyed the cool of our resting place, only now, in the approaching darkness, deciding that we should begin to move in order to reach our hotel before night.

We could hear the pilgrim a long way before we actually saw him—a heavy, slow thudding which echoed off the tarmac road out of the gathering dusk. It was late: the birds had stopped singing a while before, and the countryside was full of quiet rustlings and stirrings as it prepared itself for the night.

The thudding could perhaps have been ominous, menacing in its slowness, but there was within it a weariness that provoked only sympathy, not anxiety. As we looked, a strange shape appeared over the brow of the hill, only barely discernible as a human figure. It seemed more like some curious insect with a huge carapace, black and solid, beneath which the frail carcase staggered wearily, waving two extended limbs that dragged and clattered on the ground. As the figure drew nearer, we saw a tall slender man of late middle age, with grizzly stubble on his face and a leathery neck protruding from the open collar of his shirt in a way that only served to reinforce his likeness to a tortoise. He was using two walking poles, but clearly, even with these, he could barely support the weight of his pack. Sweat was running from his forehead, dripping into his eyes, and it was an indication of his weariness that he no longer bothered to wipe the beads of moisture from his eyelids but simply blinked them away, leaving his hands free to continue wielding his sticks.

Eleanor called out a cheery greeting in English, then another in French and again in Spanish. The man did not answer: he had clearly reached a pitch of exhaustion that prevented him from focusing on anything other than placing one foot after the other. We resumed our packing, carefully emptying the unused water back into our water bottles and wrapping up the teabag so that it could serve on another occasion.

On our arrival at the hotel, we saw the huge pack once more, now devoid of its carrier, silent and menacing in the tiled hallway. Peering into the empty dining room, we asked the hotel owner where the other pilgrim was. He shrugged eloquently and told us that he had been too tired to wait for his meal but had instead gone to his room, supplied only with bread and cheese and a bottle of beer. 'He bears too much,' said the Spaniard in broken English. 'The destination will not see him.'

In the morning, on enquiring again after the welfare of our fellow pilgrim, the hotel owner told us he was not well at all and the doctor had been called out. He shook his head in a gesture that expressed a weary familiarity with such folly: 'The pack,' he said. 'Always the pack.'

As we turned once more to the route, we shared a moment of sympathy for the stranger whose journey, so lately begun, now seemed already at an end.

It is a common and almost universal error of the first-time pilgrim to try to carry too much equipment. Partly, this is the nature of the trip itself: when a journey has been a long time in the planning, when time off has been carefully saved up, financial arrangements made and routes explored, there is plenty of time to gather endless bits and pieces that might come in useful on the journey. Pocket sewing kits for emergency repairs, binoculars for bird spotting, and a book on bird recognition in case we can't identify them once we have spotted them—all too soon, the heap of things waiting to be packed carefully into our purpose-bought, brand new rucksack, with its many pockets and useful attachments, has attained mountainous proportions. Added to this is the undeniable attraction of apparently vital pieces of kit without which no expedition can hope for success—specially manufactured technical items designed to appeal to the 'kit-junkie' who lurks within every aspiring pilgrim, carrying the faint promise that its purchase is all that is necessary to ensure a successful, rapid, pain-free journey.

How proudly does the first-time pilgrim set off on the first day of their adventure, secure in the knowledge that they have foreseen every eventuality and packed something to protect against it! How soon does pride become despair as the weight of the pack digs into tender shoulder blades, rubs against fleshy hips and presses down upon feet not yet hardened to the rigours of the road! A heavy pack makes the journey slower. A heavy pack encourages blisters. A heavy pack is in danger of provoking the very incidents from which it is supposed to protect the traveller, as longer journey times lead to greater fatigue and greater risk of accident. It is far safer, easier and happier to travel light!

There are, undeniably, some pieces of equipment without which it is positively foolish to travel—waterproofs, spare food and drink, a first aid kit being only the first stage. As a rule of thumb, the received wisdom of carrying no more than 10–15% of your body weight is a good starting point, although, if you are very small and slight, this might be a figure that you cannot achieve.

After 20 years of pilgrimage on foot through the UK and Europe, I believe I have got the process of packing a rucksack down to a fine art. The basics for safety are followed by a minimum amount of spare clothing, a mobile phone and charger, Earl Grey teabags (they never taste the same in other countries) and plenty of my favourite brand of blister plasters. These items are packed in separate waterproof bags, topped off with emergency chocolate and water. I pride myself on the lightness of my pack and rejoice when I can walk gaily uphill, past other more heavily laden pilgrims. However, even with my 7 kg pack, I am put to shame by my daughter and fellow pilgrim, who carries practically nothing, avowing that she remains light in spirit and heart because she is light in clothes and kit.

Eleanor's ability to travel light is down to three things, I believe. First, she has never been much of a materialist, preferring not to clutter up her life with physical possessions. She is not seduced (as I am) by the claims of the latest piece of technical kit or clothing, however featherlight and essential it promises to be. She is curiously unattracted to the latest, best model of water container / blister plaster / solar-powered phone charger, preferring instead her familiar well-tried kit. She does not need this year's model of technical clothing. Content that she has proved herself to be a real pilgrim by virtue of the number of miles she has already travelled, she does not feel she must show off her level of expertise to fellow travellers through her gear or her attitude. So she is happy to take a back seat in the discussions over 'wicking' clothing or the value of silver as an antibacterial agent.

The second reason behind Eleanor's gift for travelling light lies in the confidence she has in her own ability as a pilgrim. Developed over many journeys, supplemented by her hobbies of running and weight training, she does not have to bring items of equipment with her in case of an imagined or anxiously predicted disaster. She is confident instead that she carries within herself all that she needs to meet the events of the journey. She is fit, optimistic and resourceful. She believes in the essential goodness of human beings and has a first aid qualification. She trusts herself and therefore has no need to place her trust in an external object.

Finally, Eleanor has made all her pilgrimages with me, her mother. She knows that whatever disaster may occur, whatever situation threatens, I will be with her and she can rely on me to help her find her way through it all. So her pack is light and mine is heavier because in mine is all that she might need as well!

These hard-learnt lessons of the imperative of carrying only the very basics necessary for a safe and successful journey can be carried with equal emphasis into our lives off the road. In these times of material overload, where purchases can be made from anywhere with an ease that was unthinkable only a decade ago, the dangers of becoming submerged by physical objects is acute and real. Wherever we turn, our senses are assaulted by advertisements pressing us to buy something, seducing us into believing that our lives could become better, easier, more meaningful if only we purchased a particular object, wore a certain garment or ate the latest superfood. Our intimate relationship with the internet means that our buying habits can be monitored, enabling greater accuracy on the part of aspiring vendors in targeting our most vulnerable places, aiming ever more precisely at the heart of our insecurity, convincing us ever more eloquently that our lives will only be complete after this last purchase.

One of the real gifts of pilgrimage is that, for a time at least, we are distanced from this constant attack by the agents of materialism. Once packed, we are forced to consider most carefully before taking on any further burdens, aware that each additional object is a threat to our success as pilgrims. The same lesson can be applied to our lives on our return home: after weeks spent living out of a backpack, carrying all that is necessary in one small container, we look with fresh eyes on the clutter of objects that surround us in our homes and our lives. It can be very rewarding to make use of these fresh eyes, surprised by surfeit.

In a similar way, the emotional lessons of the unburdened pilgrim can be applied to our daily lives. One of the many reasons that people give for going on pilgrimage is the opportunity to leave behind the anxieties and preoccupations of their day-to-day existence. We may not recognise the heavy burden of our responsibilities and our worries, the tangle of emotions that weigh us down (positive thoughts as well as negative ones), the turbulent thoughts and constant nagging feeling that there is something else, something more we should be doing. The lightness of heart that expresses itself in laughter and conversation, animated encounter and earnest discussion, can be the pilgrim's most unexpected blessing on their journey. This lightness comes from the realisation that, for a short space of time, nothing more is required of us as human beings than that we should behave responsibly towards the environment, caringly with our fellow pilgrims and lovingly towards ourselves.

The first-time pilgrim can feel alarmed by the absence of emotional concerns that, for so long, have been their daily companions. It can feel selfish to be worrying about nothing more serious than where the next café stop will be or what the evening's accommodation will be like. But a short break from duties and obligations can enable rest and recreation to effect healing and restoration of strength. It can mean that we are in a better place to take up our responsibilities and concerns on our return home, with the memory of carefree times available as a source to draw upon.

A time away from everyday life can also enable us to discern more clearly which of those emotional burdens and responsibilities we should be shouldering and which are simply not necessary. Too often, we continue to take upon ourselves the cares and problems that should not be our concern. Too often, we continue to feel obliged to undertake tasks and assume roles that are no longer necessary: the subject of our preoccupations may not need the same level of care as it once did, or the situation may have changed and developed. Sometimes it takes a time away to be able to see clearly. The act of distancing ourselves from the events of our normal outline gives us a sense of perspective that may usually be lacking. A determination to assume, on our return, only those responsibilities that are legitimate and important, both to us and others, can be a very valuable decision to emerge from a pilgrim journey.

For some pilgrims, the stripping away of physical possessions can produce a real anxiety. The fear that we are, after all, only as valuable as our accumulated material goods can be very disabling. For those who have equated their sense of self with the amount of wealth and property they own, the art of living without being surrounded by those protective possessions can be threatening indeed. What if we are judged and found wanting? What if, without our defensive wall of 'stuff', there is nothing at all? This anxiety can also attack those whose sense of worth lies in the number of people or causes they feel responsible towards. A lack of self-esteem can be disguised by a fervent espousal of the needs of others. A failure of self-love can be buried in a constant need to care for others.

Time spent alone on the road with only ourselves for company can seem threatening indeed. But it is out of this that the realisation of God's love for us can come. From the dark fear of nothingness, the fact of the high value that God places upon every single one of us shines like light. 'Are not two sparrows sold for a penny? Yet not one of them will fall to the ground unperceived by your Father. And even the hairs of your head are all counted. So do not be afraid; you are of more value than many sparrows' (Matthew 10:29–31).

Reflection

The time immediately upon your return from a pilgrimage, however long or short the journey, can be an opportunity for seeing the things of home in a new light. Long-accepted values and assumptions can be re-examined while the lightness of physical and emotional journeying is still fresh in our minds. Try to maintain that attitude while you take time to re-examine the fixed points of your material, emotional and spiritual life and reassess their worth.

'Take no gold, or silver, or copper in your belts, no bag for your journey, or two tunics, or sandals, or a staff' (Matthew 10:9–10). Although we may have lived for many days with no more possessions than can be carried in our bags, this extreme form of physical poverty is a practice that is impractical to maintain in everyday life. However, an attitude of sitting lightly to our material goods can still be usefully cultivated.

Set aside some time on a regular basis for examining the number and type of possessions you have. You may want to take a room at a time or a type of possession—clothes or books. Examine each thing and decide whether you really need it or whether it could serve the kingdom better if it did not belong to you but to another. If you can, sell your extra possessions and give the money to your favourite charity, or, if you can give them to someone who needs them more, do that. Remember that the treasure of earth is liable to theft and corruption and that our hearts must be focused on building up treasure in heaven.

Challenging though it may seem, getting rid of the physical clutter in our lives is an easy task compared to sorting out the essentials and inessentials of our emotional lives. You may need to engage with the following reflection more than once, as your insight develops. You will need a handful of stones and a handful of hearts. The hearts can be wooden or paper, but need to look attractive to you.

Find a comfortable place to sit, at a time when you know you will not be disturbed. Taking a stone at a time, think of an emotional responsibility or concern that you have. Pray for God's wisdom in deciding whether it is a genuine responsibility or one that is now outdated or has never really been valid. For example, perhaps you are looking out for a sick neighbour who did need regular care but now needs only an occasional visit. You might be preoccupied with a child whose actions need to be acknowledged now as more their own responsibility than yours. The loving attention can still be there, but the anxious fretting can be let go. You might, however, feel that a greater degree of responsibility should be taken for ageing parents who need more care than they did previously. Perhaps an initiative in the church needs your input if it is to thrive, or maybe someone you know needs help and support through a difficult time.

Once you have divided your stones into two piles, take the stones representing those obligations and duties that are no longer current or necessary and return them to where you found them. Then, taking the stones that symbolise your current emotional burdens, ask God for the strength to carry them and the grace to turn them from burdens into joys, from responsibilities into caring partnerships, working with God and the people involved to transform the situations concerned.

As you pray, place each stone upon a heart. Then move the stones away until you are left simply with the hearts. The hearts can form part of your prayer routine. You can write the name of the person or situation on them or decorate them—or perhaps even make bunting out of them to brighten up your prayer space.

The next chapter, on Via Limovigensis, might help you to reflect on those spiritual habits that are useful and those that have become heavy or were useful previously but have now been outgrown. As the poet R.S. Thomas writes in his poem 'The kingdom', admission to the kingdom of heaven is free if we only let go of all our desires and offer instead simply our faith (*Collected Poems*, Orion, 2000).

3   Be open to God

Now as they went on their way, he entered a certain village, where a woman named Martha welcomed him into her home. She had a sister named Mary, who sat at the Lord's feet and listened to what he was saying. But Martha was distracted by her many tasks; so she came to him and asked, 'Lord, do you not care that my sister has left me to do all the work by myself? Tell her then to help me.' But the Lord answered her, 'Martha, Martha, you are worried and distracted by many things; there is need of only one thing. Mary has chosen the better part, which will not be taken away from her.'

LUKE 10:38–42

My discovery of pilgrimage was sudden and life-changing. As part of the preparation for ordination, every would-be priest is required to undertake a retreat for a number of days before the ordination service itself. I duly did this and found it to be a very difficult and challenging experience. The retreat centre was a former convent, well-appointed and reasonably comfortable, but in a semi-urban setting, next to a motorway, the noise of which prevented us from using the grounds. The retreat was in silence, punctuated only by brief talks on the theme of our approaching change of status; the rest of the time was for personal silent prayer.

Never used to silent or contemplative prayer, I found the time almost unendurable. Enforced stillness agitated my restless body, and my mind echoed my physical dis-ease. I realised that I could not live out my ministry unsupported by a method of prayer that would sustain and strengthen me. By the end of the retreat I had determined that I would find an approach to prayer that would enable me to explore and deepen my relationship with God in a way that being still and silent could not. Chancing upon an article in *The Church Times*, I decided to try pilgrimage, defined within that paper as 'a walking prayer'. My first journey, from Assisi to LaVerna in the footsteps of St Francis, made in a spirit of discovery and exploration, proved to be the start of a lifetime of adventure. It led to a gradually deepening appreciation of the spiritual benefits of undertaking a spiritual journey, whether long or short, to a place that is recognised as being sacred, whether by people in general or in the course of a personal spiritual journey. During the intervening years, I have walked throughout both Europe and the United Kingdom, and I never fail to recapture that sense of fellowship with God and my fellow human beings which is a key factor of pilgrimage. At the core of my prayer life is the call to pilgrimage, to the journey, discovering aspects of God, myself and the community in which I live in ways that would not otherwise be possible for me.

However, I have since learnt the benefit of silence and stillness, and have learnt to appreciate the gifts that they can bring. The activity and energy of pilgrimage channel a physical and mental restlessness, creating a space for reflection and spiritual conversation, but these times of movement and energy are most productive when balanced by times of contemplation.

One of the joys of being able to make a long-distance pilgrimage by foot is getting to know a country, its landscape and its local populations, in a way that is not given to the motorist. Travelling at walking pace, we can truly appreciate the nuances of the countryside. The pilgrim can observe the way that one landscape almost imperceptibly shapes and reshapes itself into a different kind, grassy slopes gradually steepening to rocky hilltops or gently smoothing out to become riverside meadows. These, in turn, may become bare plains, stretching flat in all directions, or rise again to form ridges and high trails. Settlements, too, can be experienced at close hand, the first scattering of dwellings on the outskirts of a town gradually thickening to form long rows of houses or merging into industrial landscapes before coalescing into a town centre with shops, churches and government buildings.

This is particularly true of the beginning of the long pilgrim trail which is the Via Limovigensis, an ancient route with its starting point in Burgundy, leading eventually into Spain to pick up the path to Santiago de Compostela, but first passing through the French medieval city of Limoges, from which it takes its name. From the hilltop town of Vézelay, with its beautiful church perched at the top of the highest hill, commanding views over the green Burgundian countryside, the walker spends several days in gentle countryside. Rolling hills, lush dark woods and green slopes dotted with fat cattle lie on either side of the path, which is shared with only an occasional pilgrim, since there are many miles to travel before reaching the Spanish border and the main route to Santiago de Compostela, and few pilgrims begin so far from their destination.

The villages are small and lacking in facilities, but compensation is found in the hospitality of the villagers themselves, who offer water and shelter to weary walkers. Places to stay are few in number and, to begin with, are small hotels rather than traditional hostels. Pilgrims must plan their days carefully so that they may arrive at these stopping places, for there are no alternatives. Gradually, however, as the route goes further south, the number of villages increases, and larger towns and cities soon begin to appear on the map—ancient settlements whose narrow cobbled streets are lined with crooked, wood-beamed houses, the top storeys overhanging the lower ones.

These towns are dominated by their churches. Later municipal architecture cannot begin to overshadow the soaring towers and solid stonework of the cathedrals of Bourges and Limoges, the vast church of Saint-Léonard-de-Noblat, or even the churches in smaller towns such as Bénévent-l'Abbaye and La Souterraine. There, pilgrims who have experienced the deep solitude of the Burgundian forests may feel relieved and pleased to be connected once more to their fellow human beings, secure in the knowledge that this, too, will pass as the route leads from the centre of crowded streets to open countryside once more.

With its times of quiet and intervals of urban clamour, a balance is achieved by the route, which provokes a similar feeling of balance within the mind of the pilgrim. Just as walkers can benefit from the different landscapes through which they journey, so too can the spiritual pilgrim draw refreshment from a variety of methods of prayer. As we change and grow, our spiritual needs, just like our physical and emotional needs, will also develop and change over the years. As our relationship with God deepens, we may find that our initial habits of prayer and reflection no longer sustain us. Times of challenge and difficulty may require another way of tapping into the support of comfort that we require. Slower periods can cause us to find that a previously satisfactory prayer life feels stale and unrewarding. Although times of spiritual dryness and desolation inevitably form part of our spiritual journey, yet it can be fruitful and productive to reach out for and explore the many types of prayer that have been practised by those who have gone before us, building on their experience to discover new aspects of prayer for ourselves.

However, we must be mindful that new ventures into prayer are best undertaken within the context of a balanced and regular pattern of prayer and spiritual exercise. The pilgrim who encounters daily changing landscapes, which place different demands upon the body, does so within a pattern of walking and resting that is developed at a very early stage in the journey. After the initial few days of becoming accustomed to the rigours of the route, pilgrims soon find a pattern that enables them to continue the journey for as long as is necessary. This pattern will include periods of activity and of rest; it will contain occasions for refreshment and relaxation, and should be adjusted, if not exactly to the requirements of the individual, at least to the needs of the group and the availability of hospitality and accommodation. Without such a structure, it is easy to become overtired, to miss occasions for eating and resting, or to linger unnecessarily rather than make steady progress.

So, too, prayer pilgrims should set aside a regular time to listen for God's voice, to reflect on his word and to conform their hearts and minds to his will. This pattern of prayer can be specific to the individual. Efforts should be made to avoid pressure from those who would dictate the best time and place in which to pray, but to listen instead to the desire of the heart. Whether early or late, in the middle of the day or right at the end, however, do try to consecrate a part of each day to God. It is only when we do this that we are able to set priorities for our lives. Allow the prayer to set the rhythm of the day: it is from within this structure that freedom will be found to explore and experiment, taking unfamiliar turns and investigating different approaches.

As with a pilgrimage, so too with the personal spiritual journey: both can be undertaken alone or in groups. Each way offers benefits, and balance between the two is ideal. It is while walking alone that pilgrims are offered opportunities to look deep within, perhaps learning new truths about themselves or facing long-buried issues and, in the solitude, gaining understanding, acceptance and healing. The company of others, however, brings different gifts, as the viewpoint of a fellow traveller can shed new light on a problem and thus offer a further chance at resolution. Similarly, the experience of prayer alone can be enhanced by prayer with others, and the danger of over-introspection or selfishness can be offset by the sense of community drawn from fellow worshippers.

One of the challenges that pilgrims face when seeking God is actually to focus on the task itself. This is not to say that the act of prayer should be approached with a feeling of grim determination or a sense of obligation, but rather that the tendency of our minds to wander makes them easy to distract. When faced with a task that requires some concentration, almost anything can provide a path of thought that drifts away from the central aim. This is particularly the case with pilgrimage: walking through beautiful and varied landscapes, the inclination can be simply to take the opportunity to relax into a trance-like state, which is often reinforced by the rhythm of walking. Thus, many minutes can go by before the pilgrim endeavouring to pray even realises that they have allowed themselves to be distracted from their task. It is possible to deal with this issue by including the landscape within the prayer; it is also helpful to have a definite intention, for a certain amount of time, to focus and concentrate the mind and heart on communicating with God, exploring and opening a relationship with the all-powerful Creator and allowing our thoughts to realign themselves to the path of his will.

Here, again, the concept of balance is all-important, both in methods of prayer and in the choice of things to pray about. It can be helpful to write a list of subjects or ways of praying that you intend to use. If you prefer not to feel restricted in this way, simply be aware of the types of prayer that you tend to fall back on, and be ready to journey further afield from the familiar routes.

Many people find that making a pilgrimage brings great insight into the way they have acted and spoken in the past, such that they gain an understanding of the reasons for their previous behaviour and perhaps learn new ways of thinking or how to change underlying patterns. This useful exercise can prove very demanding, and care should be taken not to delve so deeply that a sense of perspective is lost and we are overcome by our own inadequacies and failures, despairing that we will be able to change. Times of confession and self-acknowledgement, therefore, should be balanced with times of looking beyond ourselves, appreciating the natural gifts with which we are surrounded, taking pleasure in the simpler things.

Walking one morning through a particularly isolated area of France, I was alarmed to discover that I had forgotten to buy food supplies for the day, counting too optimistically on finding a local store in one of the small villages along the way. By the time I reached the place where I was to stop for lunch, I was truly hungry. The tomato pasta and fresh bread that the auberge offered me formed one of the best meals I had ever tasted, eaten with relish, deeply satisfying and welcome in its simplicity.

Similarly, although we should not feel ashamed or embarrassed to include personal request in our times of prayer, too much time devoted to a personal 'shopping list' or to asking God to change the realities of our lives, so that they may become easier and more comfortable, does not achieve a great deal. Rather, it encourages us to see God as a sort of luxury department store, where, in return for offerings of praise and worship, all sorts of benefits can be ours. A willingness to allow ourselves to be moulded to Christ's will, and a readiness to accept that which cannot be changed, asking instead for the grace to make the most of the situations in which we find ourselves, may be more productive than an unarticulated yearning for a less stressful life.

It can be useful to incorporate the patterns of the day into the rhythm of our prayer life. So, for example, as the day begins we can offer thanks that we are once again able to meet it, asking that we may be given the grace to fill it with actions that are pleasing to God and beneficial to ourselves and others. We can spend some time in silence, listening for God's word, allowing ourselves to dwell in his love. In this way we will be given the courage and stamina to meet the challenges of the day ahead.

Much like Mary, who was just as aware as her sister Martha of the many tasks that were involved in offering hospitality, we may pause for a while to rest in God's presence before we begin. It is only when we have a sense of the divine perspective that we are able to discern which of the day's tasks are important and which are not; which of the things we can choose to do will benefit others and which will only satisfy ourselves; what we must do to nurture our souls and what we must put aside in order to avoid cluttering our lives with the unimportant and distracting.

Periodically, as the day is played out, we may choose to return to a time of silence, reacquainting ourselves with the depths of God's love, realigning ourselves with his will. However, we may not be permitted to spend the day in contemplation and silence, but must make contact with the world beyond our own selves. In this, too, we can bring balance and a sense of God's priorities. There is a tale told about St Francis, who went with his brother monks into a village for the day. All day long they worked side by side with the villagers, helping them in their daily tasks. Finally, as the sun set, they walked wearily back to their dwellings. One of the younger monks addressed St Francis in a worried voice: 'I thought we were going out to share the gospel.' To this the saint replied, 'If these people have not heard the gospel today, then reading from the Bible will not make any difference to them!' So, too, the necessary duties of our daily lives, which often seem so humdrum and soul-destroying, can be seen in the light of Christ's missionary work on earth as we try to ensure the comfort and peace of those around us.

If we are on physical pilgrimage, we can endeavour, with only a little effort, to ease the lives of those with whom we share the path. The offer of some water, a blister plaster or a sympathetic listening ear speak the gospel as profoundly as any spoken words, as do the passive tasks of simply making sure we leave a stopping place as we found it. Positive actions such as litter picking can result in a place being better because we have passed through it. Similarly, if our pilgrimage is an inner journey, undertaken in our place of living and working, we can resolve that the end of the day will see the world a better place because we have lived in it. Just one small action is all that is needed, for many such actions will have a huge effect and the kingdom of God will be brought one step closer.

One of the joys of pilgrimage is that it allows us to break free from our regular habits, our traditional ways of doing things. We will find ourselves, by necessity, eating food that we have not tasted before, at times that may be beyond our control, with people whose company we have not chosen. We may end up sleeping alongside strangers, unexpectedly close to people with whom we may never come into contact again. Although this enforced displacement from our comfort zone presents many challenges, it will also open our eyes and our hearts to new experiences. A food previously untried may become a new favourite, a chance encounter develop into a lifelong friendship.

One of the resolutions that can be taken from a pilgrimage experience is the determination to maintain this open-mindedness and readiness to explore and discover, once we have returned to our familiar locations and routines. So, too, we can be prepared to try new ways of praying, new paths into an encounter with God. For many of us, the default in prayer is of silence and stillness as we try to focus our hearts and minds on God. A familiar place, furnished comfortably in a way that we find helpful to prayer; a habitual posture, sitting or kneeling; a favourite Bible passage or verse—these can all lead us in. They are valuable assets to maintain and develop our prayer life, but, if we adhere to them too dogmatically, they can stifle or restrict our relationship with God.

Occasionally, it can be helpful to explore other methods of prayer, perhaps making use of all our senses in an effort to deepen and focus our thought and reflections. A favourite reading or a piece of music whose tune uplifts and inspires us, or whose words, whether secular or religious, resonate with our experiences of God; a picture or icon, again with a secular or sacred subject, that provides a springboard for our prayers; incense or scented candles whose fragrance reminds us of particular times or helps us to worship God with our whole selves—all these can be employed in the adventure of prayer.

Holding pebbles and asking God to soften our hearts, when they have become hardened with greed and self-concern, envy and anger, reminds us of his promise that he will remove from us the heart of stone and give us a heart of flesh (Ezekiel 36:26). Wooden crosses, carved to be cradled in the palm of a hand, are a physical symbol of Christ's sacrifice for us, his liberating gift of grace and mercy. Strings of beads can draw us into the heart of payer as we recite a well-known formula, allowing its repetition to sink deep into our hearts. Nor should newer methods be disregarded, such as online prayer labyrinths or the opportunity to join in virtual services. The internet is full of opportunities for exploration and discovery, offering a huge variety of resources and help.

This richness should be treated with caution, however, lest we become bewildered by the variety and so satiated with choices that we are distracted from our original purpose. At the heart of all wandering and exploration, our restless yearnings and incoherent stumbling, there should lie a true desire to align ourselves with the will of God, whatever that means for us and whatever it brings. Only then can we make our journey in peace, confident that we are treading in the path of truth and love.

Reflection

A sensory approach to prayer can include many different methods and serves to remind us that our spiritual life and physical life are intimately connected.

Taste

Our sense of taste is a powerful one, and correct nutrition is never so crucial as when travelling on foot over challenging terrain for a sustained period of time. Too often, though, we treat food either as a method of self-indulgence or as an enemy, a forbidden temptation.

Take a piece of food that you eat every day—bread, perhaps, or an apple. Try to eat it slowly and mindfully, savouring the flavours on your tongue, focusing on the texture of the food in your mouth. Eat thankfully, aware that others in this world suffer from hunger. As you praise God for his creative goodness, for his gifts of food and drink and for your ability to enjoy them, offer a prayer for those who struggle to find essential supplies, whose lives are worn down by the effort of survival.

Smell

The sense of smell is connected to a part of our brain that is strongly linked with memory, which is why remembered scents can conjure up such powerful feelings. If you are able, buy or pick a strongly scented flower or herb—such as rosemary, mint, lilies, roses or lavender—or light a scented candle. Breathe in the scent slowly and deeply, allowing it to fill your lungs. Focus on the scent itself and the promise it carries of the beauty of God's love for each individual and for all creation.

Touch

Take time to cherish every human contact that is your privilege to make today. Appreciate the love communicated through a gesture. Be affectionate towards the people with whom you share your life; don't forget the reassurance that a hug or handshake can provide. As you greet people, pray for them, commending them to God.

Hearing

At intervals during the day, pause for a few minutes to listen to the sounds around you. Some of them will be infrequent, some continuous. Some you will find appealing, such as the song of birds or the sound of people talking; others may be jarring or irritating. Focus on one sound and listen to the sounds within it, exploring the variation of tone and pitch. Pray for the grace to listen to the world around you—its sorrow and its joys. Ask God for the grace to hear his voice speaking to you among the sounds of daily life.

Sight

Find somewhere comfortable to sit and turn your gaze upon the floor. Focus on just one small spot upon it. Look at the colours and textures of this one place, the many different ways in which light reflects upon it, the tiny marks and unevenness there. Gradually widen your gaze to include more of the floor, then slowly bring your gaze up to look at more and more of your surroundings. Notice how many different colours and shades surround you; the textures and patterns of the things with which you share your space. Allow your mind to be flooded with colour and light as you observe shapes and movement. Praise God for his creative goodness: 'For you, O Lord, have made me glad by your work; at the works of your hands I sing for joy' (Psalm 92:4).

4 Rejoice in your companions

If I speak in the tongues of mortals and of angels, but do not have love, I am a noisy gong or a clanging cymbal. And if I have prophetic powers, and understand all mysteries and all knowledge, and if I have all faith, so as to remove mountains, but do not have love, I am nothing. If I give away all my possessions, and if I hand over my body so that I may boast, but do not have love, I gain nothing.

Love is patient; love is kind; love is not envious or boastful or arrogant or rude. It does not insist on its own way; it is not irritable or resentful; it does not rejoice in wrongdoing, but rejoices in the truth. It bears all things, believes all things, hopes all things, endures all things.

Love never ends. But as for prophecies, they will come to an end; as for tongues, they will cease; as for knowledge, it will come to an end. For we know only in part, and we prophesy only in part; but when the complete comes, the partial will come to an end. When I was a child, I spoke like a child, I thought like a child, I reasoned like a child; when I became an adult, I put an end to childish ways. For now we see in a mirror, dimly, but then we will see face to face. Now I know only in part; then I will know fully, even as I have been fully known. And now faith, hope, and love abide, these three; and the greatest of these is love.

1 CORINTHIANS 13

Ye goon to Caunterbury—God yow speede,
The blisful martir quite yow youre meede!
And wel I woot, as ye goon by the weye,
Ye shapen yow to talen and to pleye;

For trewely, confort ne myrthe is noon
To ride by the weye doumb as a stoon;
Geoffrey Chaucer, *The Canterbury Tales*, Prologue, lines 770–775

Go, then, to Canterbury and God speed you! May the blessed martyr give you what you desire. And I know well, as you travel on, that you will tell good stories and amuse yourselves, for certainly there is no joy or happiness to be found in journeying silently as stones.
My own translation

In the late 14th century, at the height of the popularity of pilgrimage, the Clerk of the King's Work, Geoffrey Chaucer, wrote 24 stories purportedly told by pilgrims on their way from Southwark to Canterbury. In his Prologue he introduces the pilgrims in the group and sets the scene for the tales to come, heightening all the advantages and disadvantages of travelling in a group. A mixed bag of characters indeed are this group that set off on their shared adventure—a knight rubs shoulders with a cook, a humble priest travelling alongside the bawdy 'wife of Bath'.

Then, as now, pilgrimage was no respecter of status. Admittedly the wealthier, more highly born traveller might ride on horseback and eat good food on his arrival at the hostel or abbey that was his overnight resting place. Meanwhile, the humbler pilgrim rode a donkey or plodded patiently behind on foot, satisfying his hunger with a free handout of bread and beer, which was the duty of every abbey to provide if the pilgrim could produce his testimonial or certificate guaranteeing the authentic nature of his journey. However, the difficulties and dangers they faced were the same—bands of robbers seeking to remove all valuables from the hapless traveller; bears and wolves that roamed the more isolated parts of the route; weather conditions that could make an unprotected pilgrim fall sick or even die. All these factors, as well as the need to gather for companionship to alleviate the tedium of a long, slow journey, brought together groups of people who left behind their spouses, past behaviour and previous lives to become part of a new entity, a band of pilgrims.

Today, as in the 14th century, the nature and number of one's travelling companions can transform a journey. People still travel in groups for safety, but more often now they will band together to enjoy the freedom and extra dimension that a relationship of the road can bring. Wealth, profession, status or income matter not at all beside the walking speed, adaptability and generosity of the fellow pilgrim. A basic meal shared with a good companion who is prepared to offer physical and emotional support is far more precious than a gourmet repast with a self-absorbed or short-tempered fellow pilgrim. Once again the truth of Proverbs 15:17 is found to hold good: 'Better is a dinner of herbs where love is, than a stalled ox and hatred therewith', as the King James Bible so famously puts it.

Of course, even a dinner of herbs tastes better when eaten not only in the company of friends but in the shade of some glorious tree in an ancient churchyard, the luxuriant green grass providing a soft carpet for whatever provisions have been brought along and a comfortable place to rest after the meal has been eaten. Unfortunately, pilgrims who wish to travel in the footsteps of Chaucer may find themselves frustrated in this goal. Initially, the route is exciting and full of energy. The pilgrims might say a few prayers in Southwark Cathedral, pausing before the 19th-century stained-glass windows designed by the firm of Kempe and depicting, among others, that giant of allegorical pilgrim tales, John Bunyan, as well as Geoffrey Chaucer himself. From there they will make their way through the busiest part of London, past the famous Shard, which, despite its huge physical dominance, cannot quell the spiritual energy with which the cathedral continues to infuse that area. As the journey continues, the pilgrims find themselves buffeted by crowds, their backpacks causing inconvenience to themselves and the other pavement users—a fact that they will be told about, most vociferously.

Sadly, even as the path leaves London, the journey may not unfold in a way conducive to reflection and contemplation, since the original Pilgrim's Way follows more or less the same route as the busy A2. In fact, it should be the other way round: the A2 was undoubtedly built over the route between London and Dover, going through Canterbury before pilgrims and merchants alike set off for the Continent.

It is better, perhaps, to walk across country rather than down, leaving from Winchester and following the South Downs Way, joining the London Canterbury route at Rochester. This route, too, begins in a cathedral, where, in the shadows of the cool and airy building, homage can be paid to St Swithun, bishop of Winchester in the ninth century. He was famous for his generosity to the poor and for his posthumous miracles, but mostly for the rhyme that claims to predict the weather from prevailing conditions on St Swithun's Day (15 July).

St Swithun Day if thou dost rain
For forty days it will remain
St Swithun Day if thou be fair
For forty days 'twill rain nae more.

However, the pilgrim moves from the cathedral, in the heart of the city, very rapidly through the suburbs and then out to the gentle Hampshire countryside, following rivers through small flint villages nestling around solid, well cared-for churches. The fears generated by this route are not of being mown down by a huge juggernaut while negotiating the A2; rather, they are those nebulous anxieties generated by walking for a long time in an isolated area.

Traditionally, it was believed that more virtue was attached to a pilgrimage that was undertaken alone, but this would be of little use if the pilgrim was attacked by bandits. It was safer by far to gather a group of companions together before setting off, particularly if the route was known for its dangerous nature. So, an aspiring pilgrim might wait in a particular place until a large enough group of people had gathered to make the way safe. Although the penalties for attacking a pilgrim were more severe than those for robbing a merchant, for example, the prospect of meeting a defenceless traveller, whose purse might be full of all the money needed to undertake a voyage to the Continent and beyond, was too enticing for a brigand to be put off by the threat of an upgraded punishment. Thus, in Chaucer's story, the group of pilgrims at the inn in Southwark number 'nyne and twenty'. They are clearly not already known to each other, as they are described as having come into the fellowship 'by aventure' (by accident).

There would be other places along the road for the pilgrims to gather, one of the more remarkable being the 13th-century church of Boughton Aluph, distinguished by the large fireplace added into the south porch in the 16th century. This was built to provide warmth for pilgrims while they waited to become a sufficiently large crowd to attempt the notorious Kings Wood, haunt of violent robbers.

Today, although safety must always remain a consideration for the pilgrim, the other great benefits of walking in a group have become more significant when deciding how to make the pilgrimage and who, if anyone, to choose as your travelling companions. One of the very real blessings of travelling with a group of people is that of witnessing the wonderful acts of kindness and generosity that seem to arise as a direct consequence of the journey. The feeling of closeness, of sharing the same experience with a small group of people, can be profoundly moving.

One of the greatest kindnesses I witnessed on the road involved a group of women who took turns to walk with the slowest member of the party. They encouraged her along the route, listened to her complaints and bore patiently her bitterness at the way life had turned out for her. The speed of that disgruntled walker never increased: day after day, I would see them the last to arrive at the inn or guest house. Each morning I would overtake them, however early they set off. From far off I would see the straggling group—two women in front, waiting patiently for the slower couple to catch up. The strain of limiting one's pace to match that of someone else can be very wearing and is an act of generosity, particularly when it is raining and the night's resting place is still some miles distant.

The pace of that pilgrim never increased. However, the joy with which she accomplished the daily miles, the pleasure she gradually began to feel in the journey and the gratitude with which she came to treat those who kept her company along the way transformed not only the walker but her companions and the whole party.

Learning to practise the discipline of unselfishness can bring unexpected benefits: that which might be a burden can instead bring much pleasure. I was quite a fast walker and, from the very beginning of the day, liked to set a brisk pace, often with a view to completing my designated mileage as fast as I could so that I could stop. I envied the speed of those walkers (and there are always some, however briskly you walk) who steamed past me, arms pumping, legs eating up the miles to their destination, pausing only briefly to rehydrate and perhaps munch an energy bar or two. I wanted to be like them, powering along the route, clocking up the miles, achieving the target in as short a time as possible, improving on my personal best. Oblivious to weather conditions, regardless of the towns and villages that were successfully navigated, these walkers always arrived early at their chosen destination, often having accomplished twice as much as those lesser, slower walkers who would be forced to take the bottom bunk and wait patiently for the shower to become free. The more pilgrimages I made, the fitter I became, seeking always a place among the top-ranking walkers, viewing with satisfaction the backs of other pilgrims as I gradually approached, drew alongside and then passed them.

Then, one momentous Easter, I took the whole family with me. I learnt a lot about my family on that trip—and more about myself. A pilgrimage undertaken with other people is a completely different experience. Vanished is the freedom to go from rolling out of bed to being on the road in less than 15 minutes. Instead, endless patience is required as small children are coaxed into clothes still damp from being rinsed out the night before, socks are retrieved from all four corners of the room and the large number of apparently essential items, such as teddy bears, pet rocks and favourite books, are stuffed back into rucksacks.

A group has to eat more often than a single person, and at times that are convenient to all rather than the personal preference of just one. Feet must be enquired after, tired legs coaxed along and stories invented to while away the hours before the next break. Variations in the steepness of hillsides that pass unnoticed beneath travel-hardened, speeding feet require preparation and encouragement. Previously unnoticed changes in the weather become major events as the group is halted and either sun hats and sun cream are applied or raincoats extracted and put on. Then comes the process of finding all the objects that have come out with the raincoat and are now scattered all over the path, and returning them to the pack. Gone, too, is the satisfaction of seeing the number of miles walked rapidly increasing, as the average group travels at about two miles an hour—not including stops.

However, all these minor annoyances paled into insignificance beside the wonder and delight that the whole family experienced, walking together on that first journey. I have had the privilege of repeating it many times since, on my journeys not only with my family but also with groups both small and large. Many wonderful possibilities open up when the completion of a serious number of miles each day is no longer the primary goal. When I walked from Winchester to Canterbury with my husband and youngest children, we stopped at every children's playground along the way, rediscovering the joy of swinging high into the air, and the sense of achievement in completing a set of monkey bars. We also learnt that adults really do feel sick if they spend too much time on a roundabout!

As well as the rediscovery of the lost joys of childhood came the opportunity to learn about the children themselves. Long hours spent walking and talking led to wide-ranging conversations and an opportunity to connect very deeply with each other. Walking in groups continues to offer this amazing gift. The pilgrim who joins with others, whether it is a party drawn together from all over the country on a tour, a group organised by a church or walking club, or a random collection of people walking at the same pace along the same route, will soon learn all sorts of things they had not previously imagined.

Some of these encounters can be deeply interesting: I walked for part of a pilgrimage with a man who had been responsible for the traffic systems in a major city—a fascinating and challenging job. Other chance companions can be truly life-enriching. While I was walking through the middle of France early one summer, I had the privilege of spending a day with one of the most skilled naturalists I had ever met. As we walked, he not only named the flowers and trees that made up our landscape, but discoursed knowledgeably about their life cycles, their preferred habitats and their place within the local ecosystem. My fellow pilgrim made me crouch right down to examine species of lichen—tiny frail plants apparently painted on to the surface of rocks and stones. We lay on our backs and gazed up into the trees, scouring the canopy for birds and animals. We sat patiently on the banks of rivers, watching the life in the water beneath. We journeyed very few miles that day, and I had to leave him behind and walk far into the night to reach the hostel I had booked for my stay, but it was worth it.

However, not everyone will bring joy to your journey. Inevitably, there will be those whose manner or character clashes with yours, causing you annoyance or even distress. This can be the case particularly when walking in a group, when the options of speeding up, slowing down or even taking another route in order to avoid further engagement will not be open to you. Then, perhaps, the greatest gift will be yours, requiring the greatest grace—the gift of determining to live well with those with whom you share your life, however temporarily. Small gestures of self-sacrifice—listening to the conversation of someone you find tedious or annoying—can bring great reward as, with God's help, your ability to find good in everyone is stretched and developed.

The challenges of walking together, sharing even a part of one's life with others, even for a short time, are not new. *The Book of Margery Kempe*, a 15th-century pilgrim's diary, describes how Margery irritated her fellow pilgrims so much that they even reached the point of trying to leave her behind, only allowing her to remain with the party if she sat at a different table so that she could not disturb them with her habit of praying constantly out loud. Chaucer's wife of Bath upsets the sensibilities of the more precious travellers in *The Canterbury Tales*, reminding us of the difficulties and challenges facing pilgrims in groups throughout the ages. Still, the richness of variety of background and experience that each pilgrim brings to the group can only enhance the experience and add to the lessons learnt on the journey.

So, too, must the disciples have learnt not only from Jesus but from each other. A mixed bag indeed they were, numbering fishermen and tax collectors, the educated and the illiterate, those who had travelled and those who perhaps had never left the shores of the lake that was both their home and the source of their livelihood. We know there were arguments among them: James and John, in particular, seem to have caused irritation, raising annoying questions of hierarchy in Mark 10:35–41. Again and again, Jesus showed extreme patience, encouraging them, teaching them and helping them to work together for the kingdom.

It is interesting to wonder, also, how Paul came by the depths of experience from which he wrote the famous passage of 1 Corinthians 13. How many hours of thought and reflection he must have needed, to arrive at his list of the characteristics of love—hours spent, perhaps, journeying with his companions Timothy, Barnabas and others, travelling from town to town on foot, sharing all the hardships and privations of a nomadic life. How adaptable Paul must have learnt to be as he depended on others for food and shelter, working where he could but relying on the gifts of other Christians in nearby towns when no work was available. Only from the depths of hard-learnt lessons could the music of his words have arisen: 'And now faith, hope, and love abide, these three; and the greatest of these is love' (v. 13).

These precious lessons in gracious living, so hard won by life on the road, can and should be applied equally to life after the pilgrimage, when the daily routine has once again been taken up and the familiar conversations and exchanges are renewed. Communities are valuable but fragile entities; a hasty word or impatient remark can cause rifts and disturb the balance of the life of a church or home for many days or even longer. Resentments can, if held on to, reach disproportionate levels, poisoning an entire community, causing divisions that take much time and effort to heal. Better to prevent such breakdowns by pledging to hold at the centre of one's communal life the praise of faith, hope and love.

We must have faith in ourselves and each other—the faith that is willing to look beyond the surface appearance of a personality or character and try to see what is precious in the soul beneath. Just as God gazes upon each one of us with the eyes of love, so we must learn to trust in the God who created each one of us and in the essential beauty of his creations. We must have hope that together we can build a community, a group, a family, a church, which draws ever closer to the kingdom of God, living out Christian values and sharing the hope of redemption with those we meet.

Above all, as Paul reminds us so eloquently, we must love with our whole hearts, sometimes despite our inclinations, however challenging the task appears. We must learn to love courageously, holding nothing back, acknowledging our own faults and weakness as well as recognising those of others. We must be prepared to continue to love, to learn to love, to understand and appreciate others ever more deeply, in the name of the one who loved us first.

Reflection

In 1889, at the age of 15, Thérèse Martin entered a convent in Lisieux, Normandy, and took for herself the name 'Thérèse of the Child Jesus and the Holy Face'. She spent all her life there, dying of tuberculosis at the age of 24, unknown by other than her fellow nuns and her family. So she would have remained but for the publication of her autobiography, *Story of a Soul*, in 1898. This simple, somewhat sentimental tale became immediately popular; she was canonised, made a Doctor of the Church, and is today one of the most popular of the saints.

Her knowledge of life was narrow but deep. What she brought to those seeking spiritual enlightenment was an awareness of the challenges of living in community, dedicating her life to a sacrificial love that encompassed all around her. She practised the 'little way' of small acts of kindness to those around her in the name of Christ, and of the redemption of the human race. 'My vocation is love,' she wrote, and she tried to obey Christ's command to love one another to the maximum of her abilities. A Carmelite priory contained no threats to life or health from fellow nuns, but she suffered, as do all who share their life in any way with others, from hostile negative feelings from and for those around her. 'Miss no single opportunity of making some small sacrifice, here by a smiling look, there by a kindly work, always doing the small thing right and doing it all for love,' she wrote, never forgetting that all her efforts at love were nothing without God, the originator of all love. She learnt most painfully the cost of love: 'I know now that true love consists in bearing all our neighbours' defects, not being surprised at their weakness but edified at their smallest virtues.'

We, too, can join in the task of Thérèse of Lisieux in changing the world one small step at a time. Acts of kindness don't have to be great things affecting many people; they may be, simply, generous acts towards those with whom we share our lives. Today there are many programmes that link in with this concept. The '40 Acts' movement, for example, invites us to 'Do Lent generously': it suggests different levels of generosity, from actions that take little time and cost nothing, such as visiting a local shop, to those that require time and commitment to bring to fruition, such as exploring the Fairtrade movement. A quick search of the internet or the local bookshop will result in many other suggestions.

If it is not possible to join with one of these programmes, we can simply make a vow to perform an act of kindness every day. Such acts can be practical or spiritual, such as extending a helping hand to a neighbour, or offering a surprise gift, a compliment or simply a prayer for a stranger whom you pass on the streets. If you wish to challenge yourself more, you can focus on the people within your family or community whom you find most difficult, aiming, like St Thérèse, gradually to see beyond the aspects of their character that are challenging or hurtful, to find the beauty within, that which God sees in all of us.

As an alternative to these, or as an additional practice, you might like to perform daily acts of kindness upon yourself—a chance to read, a long bath or shower, a walk in the park, or a meeting with friends. Things that enhance your life will remind you of God's love for you and will enable you to share that love more freely with others.

5 Inhabit the moment

ST DAVID'S WAY (Holywell to Bardsey Island)

'Therefore I tell you, do not worry about your life, what you will eat or what you will drink, or about your body, what you will wear. Is not life more than food, and the body more than clothing? Look at the birds of the air; they neither sow nor reap nor gather into barns, and yet your heavenly Father feeds them. Are you not of more value than they? And can any of you by worrying add a single hour to your span of life? And why do you worry about clothing? Consider the lilies of the field, how they grow; they neither toil nor spin, yet I tell you, even Solomon in all his glory was not clothed like one of these. But if God so clothes the grass of the field, which is alive today and tomorrow is thrown into the oven, will he not much more clothe you—you of little faith? Therefore do not worry, saying, "What will we eat?" or "What will we drink?" or "What will we wear?" For it is the Gentiles who strive for all these things; and indeed your heavenly Father knows that you need all these things. But strive first for the kingdom of God and his righteousness, and all these things will be given to you as well.

'So do not worry about tomorrow, for tomorrow will bring worries of its own. Today's trouble is enough for today.'

MATTHEW 6:25–34

The North Wales Pilgrim's Way, also known as St David's Way, begins at Basingwerk Abbey, where medieval pilgrims would stay before beginning their 130-mile journey from Holywell to Bardsey Island. The route website claims that in the Middle Ages, two pilgrimages to Bardsey Island were considered 'as good as one to Rome'. Certainly, if the pilgrimage is attempted during the early part of the year, or as winter approaches, when stormy winds buffet the rocky headlands and the rain is heavy and constant, it can feel to the solitary pilgrim, battling their way along narrow paths clinging precipitously to the very cliff edges, that their life hangs in the balance. Those early pilgrims would have felt the same, making their way over steep mountain passes towards Italy and Rome, or sailing in small fragile boats through the waves across the English Channel or into the Mediterranean Sea.

However, despite the inevitable rain that must be an accepted part of the journey of any pilgrim who chooses North Wales as a route, those who venture along St David's Way will, amid the downfalls, experience moments of sheer beauty. The sun filtering through the leafy shading of the narrow lanes or dancing on the ever-changing waters of the sea, catching the crests of the waves as they lap against the rocky shores; the mists of rain fading to reveal the rugged landscape with its infinite variety of greens and browns; the tiny stone cottages hidden so deep within the folds of the hills that they are scarcely discernible from the stony soil that surrounds them—all these form the backdrop for a walk as beautiful as it is sometimes challenging.

The historical town of Holywell has been a pilgrim destination since about 660. Its claim to fame is a well dedicated to St Winifred, who was beheaded there by Caradog. The healing waters of the well attract about 30,000 pilgrims a year, even today. From there, the route winds its way through the countryside of North Wales, taking in the cathedral city of Bangor and circling the Snowdonia mountain range before making for the very edge of the North Wales coast, finally arriving at Aberdaron and a ferry-crossing to Bardsey Island. The route is very mixed. Some days are spent tramping through farmsteads, remote and isolated, surrounded by green fields flecked with sheep but scarcely populated by any other creature. Other days, the walker will find friendly cafés almost directly on the route, cheerful children with buckets and spades exploring the percussive effect of the 'Whistling Sands', and fellow walkers, many with binoculars slung round their necks, ready to spot the birds that inhabit this coastline.

Bardsey Island itself is remote and beautiful. Known as the island of 20,000 saints, its remoteness attracted refugees from the pagan Saxons, or monks wishing to join the community that lived on the island. Today it remains a popular place of pilgrimage, although its beauty can be appreciated in a different but none the less powerful way when glimpsed across the waves from the coast of the mainland, as it rises enigmatic and mysterious from the storm-tossed seas that surround it.

I walked the North Wales Coastal Path just after Easter—a time in the church's year when a deep breath is drawn, one that inhales the relief and challenge of the resurrection and exhales the austerity and wilderness of Lent. A pause is appropriate to absorb the enormity of the events of Easter, time out to focus on the implications of being an Easter people who may yet have to endure their own Good Fridays and Holy Saturdays before redeeming the promises of Sunday. A good time it is to make a reflective journey, particularly one whose environment contributes to the kaleidoscope of variety that is a pilgrimage. The weather was as I expected—a lot of rain, which not only served to highlight the importance of good waterproof clothing but also emphasised the delight of sunny periods, light breezes and a sun-warmed face. A few fierce storms provided challenge and excitement, as the path is very narrow at times, and rounding exposed headland in a howling gale made footholds problematic. The breathless anxiety this induced made the times of calm all the more miraculous—occasions when the whole earth seemed to be enjoying the moment, satisfied simply to exist, content with the experience of each minute and finding it sufficient.

It was during one of these moments of divine calm that I saw the seals. I was at the top of a cliff, having laboured slowly round and up, my feet slipping occasionally on the stony path, still wet from recent rain. By chance I looked down; suffering from vertigo, I generally found it less frightening to keep my eyes focused on the route ahead, not daring to take my gaze from the path until I was completely motionless, sure of my footholds and preferably holding on to something solid. The glance I gave the shoreline far below me was no more than that—a glance—

but from the corner of my eye I saw a strange movement that seemed to go against the gentle flow of the tide lapping against the shore. I stopped and, making sure I had a firm foothold, looked down on to the rocks below.

The sea was an unusual clear blue-green, the dark shapes of submerged rocks easily visible in the shallows. Three small black dots bobbed about in a small bay, sheltered from the rest of the sea by an almost closed circle of rocks. As I gazed more closely, the dots resolved themselves into the elongated egg-like shapes of three grey seals. I was transfixed as they continued to rest in the shallows, moving their flippers occasionally to keep their place, sometimes diving below the surface for a while—still visible as they curved and rolled before surfacing once more. One of the animals approached a low outcrop of rocks and painstakingly heaved himself on to the rough surface, the colour of his skin making it difficult to spot him against the mottled grey of the rocks themselves. There he lay, basking in the sun, enjoying, like me, a short time of peace from the day-to-day tasks of survival.

Eventually, the seal slid from his place on the rocks, the three animals swam slowly out to sea again and I resumed my walk. But for that short space of time I had been totally absorbed in the wonder of what I was seeing—a glimpse of the infinite in a moment of creation. Freed from memories of the past and concerns for the future, I had been given the gift of dwelling inside the present moment, of experiencing to the full the now, in all its intensity. In a moment of letting go, space had been created for the infinite, a strange paradox whereby it is only by concentrating on the present moment that all time can be experienced.

This way of living and thinking, this inhabiting of the present moment, is known, in the language of contemporary spirituality, as mindfulness. Claimed by many different religions and spiritualities, it seems to be most commonly linked to Buddhism, with its well-known practice of meditation and silence. This is a great shame, however, as the partnership has led many Christians to reject a valid and often extremely helpful spiritual path. The practice of mindfulness—of living in the moment, experiencing the now in all its fullness, leaving behind the past and being content to trust God with the future—is implicit throughout the Bible. We are constantly reminded that unless we still our minds, freeing them from the preoccupations of our noisy, busy, selfish world, we will have no space for God. We are taught that in setting to one side our guilt and regrets, laying down our burdens of hurt and bitterness, we will make room for God to speak to us. So Moses leaves behind the mistakes of Egypt to walk as a free man to the borders of the promised land. He is prevented from entering it only when he allows the fear of an uncertain future to overwhelm him to such a degree that he reclaims ownership of his future, refusing himself the gift of a trust in God that leads to the land of milk and honey, condemning himself to wander to the end of his life in the wilderness of faithlessness (Numbers 20:7–12).

Christian mindfulness teaches us that, by focusing on the moment, we see things as they really are, not as we fear they might become. By distancing ourselves from the frantic imaginings of our frightened selves, we can distance ourselves from negative patterns of thought and experience the present moment in all its fullness—as a gift from God. Set free from the judgement of ourselves and others, we can allow ourselves to be formed and transformed by our experience of God. When we let go of our internal commentary, we can allow God to speak to us through our experience of creation and through the life and actions of Christ.

'This is the day that the Lord has made; let us rejoice and be glad in it,' says Psalm 118:24. The psalmist exhorts us to a complete involvement in the present moment, an attitude of gratitude towards the wonders of creation that surround us every waking moment of our lives, wonders of which so often we are profoundly unaware.

The experience of pilgrimage can be a wonderful way of reminding ourselves once again of the beauties of this earth. This was brought home to me very powerfully when we travelled along a route in northern France with our six-year-old son. As a baby, James had been entirely content to travel in his pack on my back, playing with the toys we had tied on at various strategic points, laughing with his brother and sisters who walked alongside him, singing songs and dropping biscuit crumbs down the back of my neck, occasionally reaching his sticky fingers down my collar to retrieve a particularly tasty fallen morsel. By the age of three and a half, he was too heavy to carry and still too small to walk, so for a few years he stayed with his grandparents while the family journeyed. By the age of six, he was determined not to be excluded from the adventures, so we planned a short, easy route with plenty of interesting stopping points, and my parents accompanied us in a backup vehicle.

Even though we had planned only a few hours of walking per day, however, we could not even do that. It was not that James didn't have the strength or endurance. It was not that he got tired or bored—quite the opposite. He found the whole journey so interesting and exciting that he couldn't bear to pass by an invitation to explore any interesting object—a new flower, a patterned stone, a shallow stream or fallen tree. A day's trip that we had thought would take two hours took more than four—but what a trip! Each moment was filled with new discoveries as we learnt once again what it is to see through the eyes of a child. 'Unless you change and become like children,' we are told, 'you will never enter the kingdom of heaven' (Matthew 18:3). That day, the whole family saw glimpses of the kingdom, revealed to us by the joy of a small boy.

Christian mindfulness is not childishness. It doesn't demand of us that we set aside our adult skills or knowledge, our wisdom learnt through experience—more that we refuse to allow our thoughts to be shaped by negative patterns of the past or fearful images of an anticipated future. We are asked simply to see what is there and acknowledge its reality. Sometimes it is enough that we focus on our surroundings, seeing in them the intense love of God for all creation. Tiny insects, soaring buildings, raging storms and sunlit puddles all point the way to God, if we only let them. At other times we can allow the words of others to teach us to appreciate, to rejoice and to respond. 'When I look at your heavens, the work of your fingers, the moon and the stars that you have established; what are human beings that you are mindful of them, mortals that you care for them?' sings the psalmist (Psalm 8:3–4). These words are echoed by poets through the centuries, finding in God's love for all creation a reassurance of their own place within that love:

I walk, I lift up, I lift up heart, eyes,
Down all that glory in the heavens to glean our Saviour.
'Hurrahing in Harvest', Gerard Manley Hopkins (1844–89)

Mindfulness is not a fair-weather method of meditation, of making space to encounter God; nor are we taught that to ignore suffering or evil makes it go away. We are told to face up to it, to acknowledge its existence, but then to put it from us, 'for it is from within, from the human heart, that evil intentions come' (Mark 7:21). Jesus, when challenged by Satan in the wilderness, did not ignore him, but nor did he allow Satan to overcome: he swiftly saw Satan for what he was, and moved beyond him. So we may face suffering and hardships in our lives with a complete acknowledgement of their existence and effects, but without allowing them to overcome us.

Nor must we use any past experiences to project frightful outcomes, but must simply call upon God to support us. 'You have given me the shield of your salvation, and your right hand has supported me; your help has made me great,' says Psalm 18:35. G.M. Hopkins, that master of descriptive beauty, echoes this truth in his reminder that 'all things counter, original, spare, strange' can teach us of God's grace; that they were created by him to shine forth with his beauty, strange though it may seem to us. So, too, our times of suffering are not undertaken alone but in the company of Christ who will redeem all things.

Just as the technique of living in the moment helps us to leave the past and the future, so can it help us towards a clear method of decision-making. Many people undertake pilgrimages at times of crisis in their lives: they may have been made redundant or lost a partner to death or divorce, or they may be facing important decisions about their future and the pattern of the rest of their lives. Just as Jesus spent time in the desert before the beginning of his ministry, so too a time in the wilderness can help us prepare for a new phase of life, or a new and different way of living it. By taking time out, we can set aside our fixed habits of thought and reaction and look at alternatives, instead of reacting without thinking. Mindfulness encourages us to stop and reflect before speaking or acting. So, Moses, the shepherd, on his daily journey into the wilderness with his flock, took time to turn aside to the phenomenon of the burning bush and heard the words that would transform not only his future but the future of the people of Israel (Exodus 3:1–6).

Mindful decision-making is something that becomes almost second nature to the experienced pilgrim. At every junction we must pause to make sure we are going the right way. If a pilgrimage route is indicated, we must search for it and check the direction. Some routes are less well marked than others and, on these, maps must be consulted, guidebooks read and even, on occasion, compass bearings taken before a decision is reached. A wrong turning can take a pilgrim wandering many miles off course, leading to extra fatigue, more blisters and a late arrival at the night's lodgings. A hasty decision is regretted further down the road.

So too, in our daily lives, decisions taken without proper reflection, relying simply on the habits of past thought-patterns, can lead us to go off course. Time spent in reflection and prayer gives us space to reconsider our choices in the light of Christ's example. We can remember the precious space that Jesus gave to those who were intent on stoning a woman to death. While he drew in the sand, he allowed the crowd to reflect on their actions, until not one of them condemned her 'and Jesus was left alone' (John 8:1–11).

The mindful Christian can share this attitude of thoughtful distance with others, careful to offer the space in relationships that is often deeply needed by our wounded world. If, as a pilgrim group, we had hurried our young son on in his journey, allowing him no time to stop and explore the wonders that surrounded him, we too would have missed out. James would have become tired and quickly bored and an adventure would have turned into a dreary trudge, punctuated by the words, 'Are we there yet?' Instead, when we paused and listened, we all discovered a world we had forgotten, full of delights. So, the attention we pay to those with whom we share our lives will be rewarded, not only in the knowledge that we are carrying out God's will by serving others but in the discovery of new aspects of their personality that we were previously unaware of, and new joys in a friendship deepened or a relationship made more profound.

Mindful pilgrims are those who pay attention to the present moment. They refuse to allow themselves to be cluttered with the relics of past experiences or burdened with the anxieties of future incidents. Instead, they see all possibilities in the now, allowing themselves to serve God fully in each moment, giving space to God, allowing him to dwell in them and experiencing his love. 'We are God's children now' (1 John 3:2), and it is in the 'now' that we will find him. We must be aware, also, that pilgrimage gives us the time out of our daily lives to reflect on our past experiences, to learn from them and come to terms with them (see Chapter 8). So, mindful walking, while important, should not be allowed to overwhelm other equally valid gifts of pilgrimage.

Reflection

Christian mindfulness is a skill, and it requires practice to recapture the ability given to us as children to live fully in the present. To begin, set aside a part of each day for mindful walking. Begin by becoming fully aware of your body. Take time to explore the sensations in each part of your body, beginning with your toes and making your way slowly up. Feel your feet as they press on the ground: can you feel the texture of the ground through your shoes? Wriggle your toes and concentrate on how they feel in your socks, sliding against each other and the fabric of the boot. Become aware of your legs and the sensations of your muscles as they support your weight. Focus on your knees. Don't be afraid to explore any sensation of pain or discomfort you are feeling, but don't give it energy; simply acknowledge its presence and move on. Can you feel your body as it comes into contact with your clothes? How does your clothing feel—smooth or rough, hot or cool? Turn your head from side to side and become aware of the sensations in your neck and shoulders. Wriggle your arm and fingers, feeling each muscle.

As you begin to move, be aware of how your feet feel as they come into contact with the ground and then leave the earth's surface again. How do your legs feel as they stride along? Are your muscles tightening, knees bending? Are your arms swinging? Do they rub against the fabric of your jacket or shirt? How does the weather feel on your face and hands? Is it cold or hot, damp or dry?

Now take notice of your surroundings, moving your focus gradually outwards. Begin by concentrating on the ground just in front of you: notice the pattern made by earth, stones and grass. Is the grass dry and brown, or long and green? Can you see each blade, and each tiny pebble? Walking more slowly, look further about you, taking in the horizon in the distance and the huge variety of landscape in between. Notice the endless different colours and textures. Listen to the sounds, pausing to identify each one, then allowing them to form a muted accompaniment to the sound of your own footsteps. What can you smell? Are you by the sea or in the midst of a wood? Would you know your surroundings if you couldn't see but could only hear or smell? As you walk, allow yourself to praise the Creator of it all, whose love for each thing is so great, whose love is demonstrated in and through your surroundings, who waits only for the invitation to live and love in and through you. 'As the Father has loved me, so I have loved you; abide in my love' (John 15:9).

If you are not able to walk mindfully, simple breathing exercises can help you pause and dwell in the moment before resuming. Find a comfortable place to sit or stand. You may want to close your eyes in order to focus better. Now, simply concentrate on your being, allowing yourself to become aware of the air as it fills your nostrils and goes deep into your lungs. Feel your lungs fill and your chest expand. Pause and then let the air slowly leave your body. Remain focused on the sensations of breathing and allow yourself to be glad simply that you are where you are. Remember that God loves you and values you and that you are complete. You may wish to say a simple prayer with each inhalation or exhalation, breathing out Yahweh, the name of God; or breathing in on the words 'Lord Jesus Christ, Son of the living God ' and breathing out on 'Have mercy upon me'. When you feel you have allowed enough space, open your eyes and continue your journey.

From 1967 to 1978, the poet R.S. Thomas was vicar of Aberdaron Church, situated at the end of the Llyn Peninsula, with a wonderful view of Bardsey Island. His poems echo the fierce beauty of the Welsh landscape and peoples and remind us of the birth of hope within each moment.

If you can, find a copy of 'The bright field' by R.S. Thomas and read it unhurriedly to yourself. It might be helpful to read it aloud. As you read, reflect on the importance of staying in the moment, of grasping the brightness that is eternity held within the moment.

6   Tread lightly upon the earth

SENTIERO FRANCESCANO DELLA PACE
(Assisi to Gubbio)

In the beginning when God created the heavens and the earth… God said, 'Let the earth put forth vegetation: plants yielding seed, and fruit trees of every kind on earth that bear fruit with the seed in it.' And it was so… And God saw that it was good.
GENESIS 1:1, 11–12

They must have seemed a strange group, that small band of ill-assorted men, dressed in nothing more than coarse tunics, roughly tied round the middle with knotted rope, frayed and muddy at the hem, torn by brambles, worn thin in some places and crudely patched in others. On their feet were simple leather sandals, toes open to the cold and the dirt, ankles looking painfully thin and scarred above the rough footwear. Yet such sights were not all that unusual in medieval Italy. Bands of itinerant monks, pilgrims travelling to holy sites in hope of a cure or a blessing, beggars, outcasts, those fleeing from justice, soldiers seeking a patron, merchants and knights carrying out their business— all sorts of people could be spied travelling among the hills around the small Umbrian town of Assisi.

The presence of these men was not unusual, but their attitude was. They did not trudge patiently along the narrow tracks and paths that threaded up and down the countryside; nor did they look around in fear of bandits or in longing for company. They were entirely self-sufficient, looking only to each other for conversation and company—but even this was not particularly out of the ordinary. What startled the peasants working steadily in their small fields, and what scattered the birds and other creatures from their paths, was the joy. These men did not trudge or march; they almost danced, so light-footed were they. Their voices were not low in conversation or keen in lament; they soared in songs of praise. With arms lifted and voices raised, they chanted the prayers of their founder, Francis Bernadone, Brother Francis of the Friars Minor, so called because he did not want even the name to imply anything other than the most humble of groups.

The joy shared among them was not that of leisure or wealth. Sworn to abstain from all personal belongings, possessing all things in common, the friars were not allowed even to touch money. They worked for the things they needed, including food and drink—things that were often given away as soon as they had been earned, if the men saw someone in greater need. On arriving at a village, they would instantly set to work, helping those who struggled, caring for those in need, showing by their actions the love they had for their fellow human beings, a love that had its roots in a passionate and lively faith in Christ. 'Preach the gospel at all times,' admonished Brother Francis. 'If necessary, use words.'

Such a lively, joyful and generous group was bound to attract others, and indeed the Friars Minor grew rapidly from the first trio who had begun their life together by restoring one of the many crumbling chapels that lay on the outskirts of Assisi. Confining their preaching to the poor and the outcast, leaving the rich and powerful to their grand churches and finely-dressed bishops, the Brothers adopted the beggars' phrase *'pace et bene'*—'peace and goodwill'—as their own. They talked in original, down-to-earth language of the freedom to be found in a lack of possessions and the joy of surrendering to Christ, teaching by parable and story.

Francis, Bernardo da Quintavalle and Petro Di Catanio formed their brotherhood on the foundation of three Gospel passages: 'Jesus said to him, "If you wish to be perfect, go, sell your possessions, and give the money to the poor, and you will have treasure in heaven; then come, follow me"' (Matthew 19:21); 'He said to them, "Take nothing for your journey, no staff, nor bag, nor bread, nor money—not even an extra tunic"' (Luke 9:3); and 'Then he said to them all, "If any want to become my followers, let them deny themselves and take up their cross daily and follow me"' (Luke 9:23). Later, this foundation was refined and simplified: 'The rule and life of the Friars Minor is this: to observe the holy Gospel of our Lord Jesus Christ.'

It is not surprising that such a lively, joyous and generous group should grow rapidly. Caught up in the vision of God's love for all of creation, the Friars Minor soon became large enough to be organised into a regular order, although the Pope would not grant it official status, as he believed that the demands placed upon the community were too harsh. A parallel order for women was formed—the Order of Poor Clares, founded by Sister Clare, who had become convinced by Francis' preaching. By 1217, there were over 1000 members of the Friars Minor. They travelled around the countryside in pairs, bringing the good news of the gospel to those who needed to hear it most—the poor, the sick and the outcast. With a rule of life based firmly on the Gospels, grounded in daily community prayer, the Franciscans transformed the monastic way of life, bringing the cloistered monk out into the world to teach and serve.

Handing over the administration of the brotherhood to those who were more gifted in that area, Francis remained what he had always been, a man of humility and prayer. He faced many difficulties, poor health preventing him from doing much that he wished, finally retreating into a life of seclusion at La Verna, where he received the gift of the stigmata—the wounds of Christ.

In September 1224, Francis left La Verna. He knew he was dying and wanted to return to La Porziuncola, the small church where his life as a servant of Christ had truly begun. The journey, travelling by donkey and surrounded by throngs of people, took two months, and when he arrived in Assisi he spent time visiting his local brothers and friends. He was nursed by Sister Clare for almost three months, in absolute darkness, suffering from fierce headaches, burning eyes and the constantly bleeding wounds of the stigmata. Yet, it was at this time that he composed the Canticle of the Sun, a song of praise and delight in creation adapted from the canticle of Daniel and simplified so that his brothers and sisters could recite it with the childlike joy that was the common thread binding Franciscan life.

On 3 October 1226, at dusk, he died, aged 44. 'I have done my part,' he declared. 'May Christ teach you yours.'

There are few ways more powerful of taking upon ourselves the lessons in spirituality for our own lives than by walking in the footsteps of the one from whom we seek guidance. How appropriate it is for us to seek to know more about St Francis in this way, as he was himself a pilgrim, an itinerant, a travelling soul seeking God in all places. To tread the paths he trod, to experience the uncertainty and insecurity that such a journey entails, to feel the demands made upon the body by weather and to experience the physical discomforts and joys of travelling, will open up to us a deeper knowledge of the life and spirituality of the one who went before us. It is on the road that we will get to grips with the unique character of the one who lived on the road, relying on the kindness of those he met on the way and the support of his travelling companions; aware, all the time, of his ultimate reliance on the God he sought so eagerly, the Christ whose life he took as an example. But the road that we take need not be the same as that trodden by Francis all those centuries ago. Each of us has our own unique journey, our own route to walk. We must never forget that the true journey is within the soul, and this journey can be undertaken anywhere.

However, we can choose to echo our spiritual path in physical steps and to seek the companionship of St Francis for a while as we do so. This will surely bring insight and understanding.

The Sentiero Francescano della Pace is a very short path. Only 30 miles in all, it can be walked in two or three days, depending on individual stamina and fitness. It extends from Assisi, the birthplace of St Francis, to Gubbio, the site of his famous encounter with the real or symbolic 'wolf' whose ferocity terrified the inhabitants of the small town before the loving and persuasive conversation of Francis encouraged it to leave them in peace. The route winds through the Umbrian countryside with its olive tree plantations and small fields, alongside streams and over rivers, through small settlements and towns, sometimes ascending the steep hills that are a feature of the landscape around Assisi, at other times keeping to the valleys and lowland. It starts at the town gate of Assisi itself, and is best begun early in the morning, in spring time, before the sun can scorch the grass brown and make walking wearisome.

The wise pilgrim spends a day or two in Assisi before setting off, visiting the sites associated with Francis before embarking on the Sentiero from the Porta Saint Gicomo in the north-east. The little town is quickly left behind and the path becomes truly rural, offering wonderful views of Assisi as it climbs steeply upwards before descending once more into the valley, setting a pattern for the journey which is continued until the suburbs of Gubbio. Walking through thick woods with no other human beings in sight, it is easy to imagine the fear with which the inhabitants of that town viewed the 'wolf' that was famously tamed by Francis. Some stories tell of this encounter as one with a human being, a brigand; others say it was with a wild animal. Either interpretation is appropriate for a man who lived in harmony with the whole of creation, treating all living things as equal before God, at ease with the humblest beggar or the most powerful lord.

Certain it is that Francis had a special empathy with animals and birds, and tales illustrating his rapport with nature abound. Birds are reported as listening to his sermons before flying off in the shape of a cross, rabbits rescued from traps refused to leave his side, and fish that had been thrown back into the river after capture lingered by his boat, not leaving until given permission by the saint himself.

This relationship with animals becomes more significant when considered in the context of the time in which Francis lived, when patterns of land use were changing rapidly, due to a rise in the population and its subsequent need for more resources in terms of food and fuel. The invention of the horse-drawn plough meant that farming methods had become more efficient. Forests had been cleared and more land had been put under the plough. The approach to animals had changed as well: no longer were they indicators of space and wildness but were becoming, instead, commercial objects. In his relationship with nature and his deep passion for God's power and love manifested in creation, Francis broke through this pattern of utilitarianism and demonstrated another way of living in harmony with all that God had made.

Today, in these times that threaten the apparent collapse and disintegration of the natural world, worn out by the unceasing demands put upon it by the human race, it is of vital importance that we seek to adopt Francis' empathy with and attitude towards all of God's creation. We must take care to appreciate every facet of nature—the ugly, unappealing side as well as the beautiful and dramatic—because it is only in doing this that we gain a fuller and more proper appreciation of our multifaceted God.

Yet we must not simply use nature as a way of illustrating God's characteristics. We must not simply admire nature because God made it, for his creation is more than that. In each tiny seed or stone, in each giant sea or expanse of plain, the whole drama and personality of God can be found. Each particle is given its being through and with God. By understanding this, we can begin to appreciate, with Francis, some of the depth and character and imagination and love of the God who made it all.

In learning to love and understand nature, we gain an understanding not only of God but of ourselves. When we are indifferent to nature, when we allow cruelty to animals or disrespect the surroundings in which we live, then we devalue ourselves and disrespect the place we hold within the sphere of God's creations. Francis' vision was of wholeness, of interdependence, of the interconnectedness of all created things. The concept of the whole world flowing from God and drenched in God's love is a key component of Franciscan spirituality today and must be played out in a practical as well as a spiritual way in our lives.

Concern for the environment, concrete physical action and commitment to caring for our surroundings and our relationship with the creatures that inhabit them must be the physical demonstration of a belief in the oneness and uniqueness of God's creations.

Reflection

In following the steps of St Francis, we are taking on more than a traditional pilgrimage, for we are not simply journeying to a destination: the journey is as important as the destination. It is while we are travelling that we will encounter the spirit of Francis and join with him in worship.

For some, simply to make the journey will be enough. They will find, as they follow the winding pathway up hills, past small wayside shrines and through villages, that the landscape and the people and animals within it speak loudly enough to them of God's glory. Some, however, may find it helpful to stop occasionally and focus on an aspect of Francis, a characteristic of his love for God, and, by focusing, come to a deeper understating of the man and his spirituality.

The following are some suggestions of how you might use these passages on the way. They are framed on Francis' 'Canticle of the Sun', perhaps the most famous of all his writings. Written even as he approached death, the poem is full of his joy in creation and love for God and his fellow creatures. These reflections are simple, requiring no special equipment. All that you need will be found in the countryside around you, with the occasional addition of something from your backpack. They can be used in any order; indeed, some depend on a sunny day or a stream of water and may have to wait until these conditions are available.

In the simple style of Francis, these prayer activities will encourage reflection and understanding, bringing another level of insight to the journey, using the power of our imagination and the wonder of creation.

The reflections are designed not only for those who have the opportunity to tread in the steps of the saint, but also for those who wish to take a reflective journey along footpaths and routes nearer to home. The materials used are simple objects, easily collected in the course of a walk. For these particular reflections, and for meditating on the life and spirituality of St Francis, it is preferable to choose a walk in the countryside; however, if this is not possible, then any green place—park or garden—will suffice.

Indeed, it is not necessary to journey at all; we can simply allow the imagination to guide us as we join with Francis in celebrating the gift of God's creation that surrounds us all. Some of the reflections—those that require a clear sky or a dark night, for example—may not be possible to undertake at any given time. This is not important; keep the reflections to hand and, when a suitable occasion arises, pause in your everyday tasks and take a moment to reflect and rejoice in your surroundings.

The first step

Most High, all powerful, good God,
all praises be yours, all glory, all honour and all blessing.
To you alone, Most High, do they belong.
No mortal lips are worthy to pronounce your name.

However you decide to plan your journey, and whatever its length, there will come a moment when you feel that you are about to embark in the footsteps of Francis. Before you do, take a few minutes to stop and do this reflection in the style of St Julian of Norwich, a medieval English mystic who had a vision of God in which he showed his love for her and for all created things. In her vision, Julian saw a hazelnut, but the reflection would work well with any small object—a nut, a pebble or a leaf.

Hold the object in your hand. Look at it and notice how tiny it is, how insignificant. Then think to yourself that all God's love went into creating that object, that God loves it, that it is unique, that it is special to God. Marvel at the miracle that created it. Then remind yourself that God loves you, that all his love for all creation was poured out in creating you and redeeming you for his own. Wrap your hand tightly around the object, then open your hand and offer the object to God, saying the verse of Francis' Canticle of the Sun above. Put the object in your pocket or backpack, or set it down near to your seat, and set off on your journey.

Living in the light

All praise be yours with all your creatures,
especially Sir Brother Sun who brings the day, and the light
you give us through him.
How beautiful is he, how radiant is his splendour.
Of you, Most High, he is the token.

Find a patch of sunlight. If the day is very fine and hot, you may want to do this reflection at the beginning or end of the day, when the sun is not so strong. If it is raining, wait until it is dry.

Make yourself as comfortable as you can—sitting, standing or lying, whatever best meets your needs. Then close your eyes and relax your whole body, letting go of any tension there may be in you. Open your hands and stretch out your arms in a gesture of offering and of receiving. Feel the sun warm upon your face. Feel it as it reaches all parts of your body and heats them. Think of the great power of the sun, warming the earth, enabling growth, giving light. Remain still in the light, asking for nothing, doing nothing. Simply focus your mind on being alive, rejoicing in every breath you take, glad that you are able to feel the life-giving warmth of the sun. Repeat the verse of the canticle to Sir Brother Sun as many times as you like, content just to rest in the sun's warmth.

The mystery times

All praise be yours for Sister Moon and the stars.
In the heavens you have made them, bright and precious and fair.

For this reflection you must, of course, wait for a dark clear night, when everything is quiet and still and there are no human distractions. If you wish, you can find a picture of a night sky and use that, or search on the internet for a suitable nightscape. Find a position in which you can comfortably look upon the moon and the stars. Look at the shape of the moon and reflect on how much of it you can see and how much you cannot. Consider how much of God's love is surrounding you and remind yourself of the vast amount that remains unknown to you. Try to count the stars you see, and remember how many more there are that you cannot see. Think about how God made every single one of them and holds them all in his hand, just as he does us and all of his creation. Reflect on the moon's influence on the tides of the sea, constant yet ever-changing, part of the rhythms of creation, moved by forces we cannot understand yet whose power we daily witness.

Changing seasons

All praise be yours for Brother Wind and the Air
fair and stormy, all the weather's moods
by which you cherish all that you have made.

The Italian weather is changeable and unceasingly various. These changes play an integral part in the survival of the landscape: rain and wind are needed as much as sun and heat if the natural world is to grow and flourish. Indeed, too much or too little of any sort of weather brings disaster—draught or floods, crop failure and destruction. So, too, are the times and seasons of our lives, each changing, each important in their own way.

If you are undertaking a physical journey, gather bits of vegetation in different stages of growth and deterioration. Try to have at least five, from seeds and young shoots to plants in full leaf and old, dying or dead leaves and plants. If this is not possible, plants from a garden or a small potted plant will be quite adequate. Place them in front of you and consider where in your life you are. Are you a young shoot or are you already showing signs of age and decay? Think of the joys associated with each season of your life and allow yourself to anticipate the joys of the season to come.

Now reflect on your spiritual life. Are you in the same place as your physical life or are you as yet unfruitful, still a seed? Perhaps you feel your spiritual life to be dead, in need of revival. Ask God to help you blossom spiritually in whatever time of life you have reached. Thank him for the joys of your life and also for the sorrows—in themselves as important to growth and flourishing as times of gladness. Put the greenery you have been working with to one side, repeating the verse of the canticle above.

Precious elements

All praise be yours, Sister Water,
so useful, lowly, precious and pure.
All praise be yours, Brother Fire,
through whom you brighten the night.
How beautiful is he, how gay, robust and strong.
All praise be yours, Sister Earth, our mother,
who feeds us, rules us and produces various fruits
with coloured flowers and herbs.

As Sister Earth acts as the mother to creation, so she nurtures all her offspring. While we consider this, we can take the time to consider how we nurture and care for our planet. Find a plant growing in a place where it is clearly difficult to grow—in the shade of a tree, beneath a tangled hedgerow or in the cleft of a rock. Even if your journey is local or urban, it is not difficult to find struggling plants, which need help to flourish. Consider what you can do to help this plant to thrive. Water it, clear the weeds from around its roots, or add some good soil to the ground around it. As you do so, consider what other steps you can do to nurture your environment, both geographical and human.

Undertake, while on this journey, to improve the landscape in one simple way each day—by picking up litter, for example. Try also to nurture the people whom you meet along the way, through encouraging words, appreciation of their gifts or acts of kindness. As you complete each action, say the verse of praise to Sister Earth.

Challenging times

All praise for those who forgive
for love of you, and endure humility and tribulation.
Happy are those who endure them in peace.
For you, Most High, they will be crowned.

The spiritual journey is not always an easy one. We will encounter plenty of setbacks and challenges as we journey in Christ to a deeper relationship with him. It is easy to map our spiritual challenges to the physical difficulties of a pilgrimage. There will be times on the journey when the way is difficult for us. We may be feeling tired, worn out by the demands of travelling or by the discomfort of our sleeping arrangements. We may have become injured—with blisters or worse. We may be suffering from adverse weather conditions, hours of rain or burning hot sunshine making the road difficult to travel. We may merely have become wearied with the journey itself and be finding it unprofitable, dull or too stressful and demanding.

So, too, our prayer life may seem bleak and dull at times, our spiritual growth and understanding unsatisfactory. How we bear these difficulties will surely determine how much we grow and change on this journey and what new strengths we discover within us for the journey of life itself.

Facing death

All praise be yours for Sister bodily Death,
from whose embrace no mortal can escape.
Woe to those who die in mortal sin.
Happy are those she finds doing your most holy will.
The second death can do no harm to them.

Find a patch of clear dry ground and lie down on it. Close your eyes and imagine that you are approaching death. What are your regrets: which actions do you regret having done, and which do you wish you had? What experiences have you left to do, which you always thought you had time for? How important are they, now that you have no time left at all? Who do you wish to be at your bedside and what would you say to them?

Now open your eyes. Imagine that you have one day left to live. What will you do with all your regrets and unfinished business, your vocations that were unfulfilled? Write them down in order of importance.

Now recall yourself to your normal life. You do not know how long you have left to live; it could be a day or many years. In view of what you have felt, what are your priorities going to be in the future? In the face of your regrets, what are you going to change about your life in the future?

Look forward and resolve to continue your journey with an awareness of death as your companion—someone sharp-eyed yet caring, who will ensure that your priorities remain as you have decided. Learn the verse of the Canticle above, and say it at the beginning of each day for the rest of your journey.

Return

Praise and bless my God and give thanks,
and serve God with great humility.

Returning from a pilgrimage or a prolonged spiritual exercise can be a powerful and difficult experience. It can take time to settle into familiar routines and there is sometimes an unwillingness to pick up old habits, especially if you feel you have been changed by the journey. Don't rush to lose sight of those changes and their benefits. Take time to reintegrate; don't be in a hurry to share all your experiences at once, but ponder on them and give yourself time to reflect. Slowly you will become absorbed back into your everyday routine, but hopefully something about you will have changed and grown, and you will find yourself able to walk in the footsteps of Francis, wherever you are.

7   Release your burdens

THE JESUS TRAIL (Tabgha to Capernaum)

Jesus went to the Mount of Olives. Early in the morning he came again to the temple. All the people came to him and he sat down and began to teach them. The scribes and the Pharisees brought a woman who had been caught in adultery; and making her stand before all of them, they said to him, 'Teacher, this woman was caught in the very act of committing adultery. Now in the law Moses commanded us to stone such women. Now what do you say?' They said this to test him, so that they might have some charge to bring against him. Jesus bent down and wrote with his finger on the ground. When they kept on questioning him, he straightened up and said to them, 'Let anyone among you who is without sin be the first to throw a stone at her.' And once again he bent down and wrote on the ground. When they heard it, they went away, one by one, beginning with the elders; and Jesus was left alone with the woman standing before him. Jesus straightened up and said to her, 'Woman, where are they? Has no one condemned you?' She said, 'No one, sir.' And Jesus said, 'Neither do I condemn you. Go your way, and from now on do not sin again.'
JOHN 8:1–11

One of the primary reasons for undertaking the difficult, lengthy and dangerous task that was a medieval pilgrimage was to seek healing. Ill health was prevalent during the turbulent Middle Ages and medicine was very much in its infancy. Poor diet and bad sanitary conditions, coupled with the scarcity of doctors, who themselves had only a rudimentary knowledge of the working of the human body, meant that to have a feeling of complete physical well-being was a rare gift.

Burdened with sicknesses, both minor and severe, people would travel many miles to a shrine or holy place favoured by the particular saint who was associated with their problem. To kneel and pray at the tomb of a saint, to kiss their bones, perhaps, or even to spend time at the site of a famous healing, was the aim of the pilgrim, hoping that the saint would either effect a cure or be persuaded to work their influence on those who had the power of healing all illness.

However, in addition to the search for physical healing, deeper and more pressing, perhaps, lay the urge to find absolution for sins committed. These sins would mean that the offender could expect to spend many years in purgatory until being finally allowed through the gates of heaven. Worse still, some offences were so grave that, unless absolution was sought and received, the final destination of the sinner would be the depths of hell. Medieval pilgrims, burdened with guilt, fearing a punishment beyond their worst imaginings, would travel many miles and undergo great suffering in order to avoid the possibility of enduring perpetual torment.

By the eleventh century, the concept of undertaking a pilgrimage to obtain remission of sins, either by asking a particular saint to intercede on their behalf or by merit of the length and difficulties of the journey itself, had become formalised. There developed a ranking system whereby the more serious the sin, the greater the distance to be travelled before absolution could be granted, Jerusalem being the destination for the most serious (and penitent) criminals. Gradually, this became part of England's justice system, both civil and clerical. A priest could send a confessing sinner on a pilgrimage before he would grant absolution; in a civil court, a convicted criminal could be sentenced to undertake a pilgrimage to pay for his crimes. This principle was resurrected in Belgium in the early 1980s, when young offenders could be offered the choice between making the journey to Santiago de Compostela and serving their sentence in a detention centre.

For most people today, the idea of a pilgrimage of penitence is less formalised, although the desire to express repentance is often a strong driving force behind the decision to begin a pilgrimage, however unarticulated that impulse might remain. Thus, in the 2010 film *The Way*, the main character carries the ashes of his son, who had intended to make the journey to Santiago de Compostela. By carrying out the pilgrimage on his behalf, leaving handfuls of ash at significant spots and scattering the rest into the sea at Finisterre, the character expresses his regret at the disintegration of the father–son relationship and tries, through his actions, to make amends.

The rhythm of walking has a calming effect upon the brain, enabling thinking to become clearer. Time spent alone for long periods gives the opportunity to reflect deeply; new places visited encourage new ways of thinking as the mind leaves its familiar paths and explores past events from a different viewpoint. I have met newly divorced men who walk fast and with concentration, expressing in their speed their anger and sense of failure over the breakdown of a relationship. They talk quickly, too, more briskly than others, and are likely at the start of a journey to be brusque and impatient with slower members of a party. Gradually, however, the journey makes its effect felt: the pace slows; the words become less harsh, more thoughtful. The judgemental critic from the beginning of the trip becomes a reflective traveller who gains insight and, hopefully, even the grace to seek amends for past actions and move positively into the future.

For some, the difficulties of the journey are part of the punishment for wrongs committed, offences against others for which great guilt is felt. Some of these pilgrims almost relish the rain, the aching limbs and the blisters, as they feel that in this way they are being punished for the things they have done. Here, too, fellow travellers hope that this impulse for self-harm will diminish over time and that a gentler, more understanding approach to oneself and one's faults will emerge, as well as a desire to make amends in a more positive way.

Others see the challenges of the route as a way of cleansing themselves from the effects of an unhealthy lifestyle—unwise life choices, poor diet, lack of exercise—which might somehow be exorcised by the difficulties of the route. These travellers, too, may find the forgiveness they seek, either in the healing beauty of the landscape through which they journey or through the generosity of those they meet on the route, bringing an openness and acceptance that may have been previously lacking.

Certainly, those who seek expiation for their guilt could do worse than choose even a short section of the Jesus Trail, the 62-kilometre trail that leads from Nazareth to Capernaum in Israel. The harsh landscape and often relentless climate can provide challenges for even the fittest walker. But there is far more to this pilgrimage than simply a masochistic desire to experience desert conditions in a land which, even today, has security issues. The trail leads from the home of Jesus through some of the sites of the most famous stories in the world, bordering the Sea of Galilee and providing a glimpse of the landscape that lies behind the Gospels.

From the very first days of Christianity, the desire to place one's own feet in the footsteps of Christ, to see and touch the buildings and landscapes that were inhabited by Jesus, has been a powerful force. In AD326, Helena, mother of St Augustine, travelled to the Holy Land and returned, just as the contemporary pilgrim will almost certainly do, laden with souvenirs of her trip. However, Helena's souvenirs were relics of saints, some fragments of the true cross, a nail from the crucifixion and two thorns from the crown of thorns. These sparked an interest in holy relics which lasted for hundreds of years, as it was believed that they retained some of the holiness of the individual with whom they were associated, as well as the healing properties mentioned earlier. By 385, the first pilgrim guide book, *Peregrinatio Egeria*, detailing the journey of Egeria in the Holy Land, had been written, and the sites mentioned in the Bible have been visited ever since.

I have to admit that I had long held out against the appeal of a pilgrimage in Israel. For me, the Gospel stories were all that I needed to feed my imagination. I did not need to see the places where Jesus told his stories or performed his miracles in order to believe in them.

In fact, I thought it might actively harm my faith if these places proved less compelling than they were in the pages of the Bible. Then, one spring, I was offered the opportunity to accompany a short tour to the Sea of Galilee and, encouraged by my husband, who thought I would be daft to turn it down, travelled to the Pilgerhaus at Tabgha to spend a week immersing myself in the landscape and stories that surround the Sea of Galilee. I remained unconvinced until the moment when my feet felt the waves of the lake lapping against them, the sun warm on my back, the only sounds the cries of the strange and beautiful birds that made their home along the lake shore. Then, the immensity of where I was, that I was truly in the land of the Bible, filled me with awe and a sense of gratitude for the privilege of being there, which has not left me since.

The Jesus Trail itself is not long, but it embraces places that resonate with the character of Christ. To stand at the top of the Mount of Beatitudes, looking out over the hills to the blue of the Sea of Galilee is to align oneself not only with those first listeners, eager to hear this strange man who was full of the language of God and a new reality, but with the hundreds of thousands of pilgrims through the centuries who have made that same journey. Seekers of truth, people of faith, they have all walked that hilltop and heard again the words that turned the world upside down, words of freedom and grace, love and unconditional forgiveness.

The pilgrim begins at Nazareth and its most prominent landmark, the Basilica of the Annunciation, where Mary first heard the angel's words that would change her life and the lives of countless millions through the centuries. Travelling along dusty tracks and roads, the walker stops at Tabgha to admire the mosaic of the loaves and fishes, which commemorates the miraculous event that happened there, continuing on to Capernaum to visit the temple and hear again of the healing that took place in that small town. But perhaps most powerful of all is the small Franciscan church, built right up against the shore of the lake, surrounded by a slightly undertended garden with a whimsical statue, leading to the gravelled lakeside. Like the other sites identified as having a connection with the life and ministry of Christ, the church and its small beach are visited by hundreds of people a day. At intervals, a coachload of chattering visitors will disgorge itself and spend perhaps five or ten minutes walking rapidly down to the lake, taking photographs all the time, before pausing briefly in the church, taking more photographs and leaving for the next destination.

However, in the intervals between these tidal waves of tourists, it is possible to find the peace that surrounds this small grey building and the waters lapping at its foundations. To sit on one of the rocky outcrops, far enough from the path to remain undisturbed even when the beach is at its busiest, with eyes on the waters that were so much a part of Jesus' life, is to experience the calm of God's love, the certainty of his grace.

It is here that Jesus met Peter and some of the other disciples after the resurrection. Having fished all night and caught nothing, the fishermen hear a call from a stranger on the shoreline, telling them to try putting their nets out from the other side of the boat. Following some strange compulsion, these seasoned fishermen obey the stranger and are rewarded with a net-breaking catch—a catch of fish to rival the one that first led Peter to Jesus three years and so many miracles previously. When Peter is told by John, 'It is the Lord', he can wait no longer in his desire to see Jesus once again, but plunges headlong into the waters of the lake, splashing towards the shoreline, leaving the others to follow with the boat, slowed down by the weight of their catch.

A wonderful reunion meal follows—a feast of bread and freshly grilled fish cooked over a charcoal fire. Undoubtedly, it is a time of joy and laughter, and yet perhaps Peter is not completely at his ease. For the last time he saw Jesus, it was in the grip of the Roman soldiers who had come to arrest him, that terrible night of the Passover. Instead of standing shoulder to shoulder with his Messiah, Peter acted rashly, cutting off the ear of one of the soldiers, escaping the possibility of drawing down fierce retribution upon them all only through the healing action of Jesus. Instead of declaring his support for the Son of God, Peter ran away, following the action at a distance, hiding in the shadows. Finally, when challenged again and again, Peter's nerve broke and he denied all knowledge of the Saviour.

What guilt must he have been tormented by! How he must have wished he could relive those final hours, change his actions and make his life both infinitely more difficult and yet much easier, since the agonies of the flesh could not have competed with the storm of self-recrimination and regret that he suffered during the dreadful hours of darkness and crucifixion. Even the news of the resurrection would not have wiped the slate clean: what could he say to make things right again? And now, here is Peter, once again with the Lord, sharing food and drink as if nothing has happened. But Peter is trapped by his burden of guilt and cannot move past it without help. It is at that moment that Jesus turns to him and, with infinite tenderness, charges him with looking after all those who will follow after him. As a shepherd cares for his flock, leading it through the dangerous parts of the countryside to safety, ensuring it is nourished and content, so Peter is to have responsibility for the community of believers that will grow and spread throughout the entire world.

Three times Peter is given this duty, the three times cancelling out those three dreadful betrayals, redeeming them, transforming them. Through error and sin, cowardice and misunderstanding, Peter has grown to be the leader of all who follow Christ. Freely forgiven of all his sins, Peter will live up to his title, 'The Rock', becoming the head of the apostles and the whole Church.

What a gift this must have been to Peter! He was no longer trapped in his own guilt but released from a past of regret and a future of sufferings. With what joy must he have taken upon himself the duties given to him by his dear Master, whom he had tried so hard to follow—tried, yet failed! Despite this failure (or because of it, perhaps), it falls to Peter to establish the Church, the body of Christ, which will carry out the task of loving the world and showing it the path of redemption to all people.

No doubt, Peter's abilities were challenged in the dreadful, difficult years that were to follow, years in which the church grew rapidly yet faced all manner of difficulties and threats. No doubt, Peter often came to wonder if he could possibly continue to shoulder the burden of leadership, but he remained faithful to the end, even, according to legend, choosing to be crucified upside down because he felt he was unworthy to be martyred in the same position as that taken by Christ at his death. The very fact of his failure, his dreadful betrayal, may have been the source of his strength. To have plumbed the depths of guilt and remorse means being in a position to understand the regrets of others. To have experienced true and complete forgiveness liberates us to forgive others just as freely.

In his powerful and moving book, *Falling Upward*, Richard Rohr explores the role of failure in our lives. He argues that it is only through the experience of allure and loss that we can truly learn to live: those who have gone 'down' are the only ones who understand 'up'. The lessons of failure, the experience of betrayal, regret and remorse, enable us to acknowledge our errors, seek repentance and experience redemption. It is only when we come face to face with our true selves and acknowledge them that we can move beyond ourselves to a new realm of understanding.

The first step of a pilgrimage is often the hardest. So much thought and preparation has led up to this moment, so much anticipation focused on one particular moment. But, in order to reach the end, we must first begin. So, if we are seeking to experience forgiveness in order to forgive and to feel forgiven, we must consciously set our faces to beginning that long and difficult journey. Too often, we think that if we hide away from our errors or bury our resentment at the deeds committed against us, we will be able to avoid the consequences of these actions. Too often, instead of fading into significance as we hope, our awareness of unresolved issues grows and develops until it obscures our relationship with the past, distorts our view of the present and blocks our vision of the future. To find forgiveness, we must first reach the point where we realise that forgiveness is needed, and this too can be a long and difficult journey.

The woman caught in adultery did not need to remind herself that she had committed a sin. The whole religious leadership had brought the matter to her attention and were determined to bring her to account over it. She was to be punished according to the law—stoned to death, dealt with righteously in accordance with Jewish tradition. But we are not concerned with the woman in this passage. She is not the main player, unlikely though that seems at first. As usual with Jesus, it is not the obvious to which we must turn our face, but the unnoticed. Jesus is here not to preserve the order of things but to re-examine previously unquestioned ways of acting and being, in the light of his saving presence. So, the crowd on the periphery of the story is where the action happens, where the transformation occurs.

In the time of silence between word and deed, Jesus waits patiently, filling the space with his love, allowing all time to expand beyond the universe as the consciousness of the world effects a paradigm shift, from justice to mercy, from condemnation to understanding, from placing the blame on others to accepting responsibility for our own sins. The woman is set free to go her way, but so is the crowd, freed from the need to convict, from a consciousness of others but an unconsciousness of self. They are delivered to a new, Spirit-filled place where forgiveness and redemption is a fact, not just a possibility.

This freedom may seem almost impossible to those of us who are trapped by guilt or struggling to find the grace to forgive those who have hurt us, sometimes so seriously that we are not sure we will even be able to survive. Perhaps all we can do is wait and pray, with faith that we will live through the 'between' time, the Holy Saturday when all is dark and time itself seems suspended. It is only in the dark that seeds can be germinated, only during times when light is absent that growth can begin. Sometimes, all that is necessary is to keep our faces turned towards the light, trusting that it will shine upon us, believing that while we wait in darkness we do not wait alone. We may not be able to see our companion, but we may trust that he is by our side.

In the silence of a small stony beach by the side of an insignificant lake, the Son of God reached out to a sinner and offered his forgiveness. In the silence of a vengeful crowd, full of a sense of its own righteousness, the son of a carpenter reflected each man's soul, offering the chance of self-recognition and transformation. It is in the silence of the journey, hours or days set aside for prayer and reflection, that we may be given the grace to look upon our own hearts in love, allowing that love to heal us and our relationship with others.

Reflection

This short reflection invites us to put ourselves in the story of Christ's forgiving love. Allow yourself plenty of time and space to engage with it, making sure you are in a comfortable place where you won't be disturbed.

Imagine you are walking along a pathway. Your route has been through a green landscape, sheltered by hills sloping gently to a grassy meadow. You have been walking along a riverbank, where cool water has kept you company with its splashing and refreshed you when you were thirsty. Gradually, however, the landscape began to change. You don't know when it happened: it seemed a subtle process, the green of the grass fading slowly to brown, the hills becoming steeper and rockier. The river, too, first became sluggish and slow, sliding sullenly at the bottom of the riverbed before it dried up completely, leaving only the memory of water. Now, you are walking through a dry and dusty landscape.

Your pace has slowed, not only because you are thirsty but because you are carrying two heavy burdens, one in each hand. You can't remember how they got there, but you can't remember being without them, either; you are only vaguely conscious of a time before, when your steps were light. Your pace breaks. The burdens are becoming heavier; it is becoming more difficult to move along the path.

The bags are not full of stones or books or any material object. The bag in your right hand is full of your regrets over your past. It is crammed to the brim with pain over missed opportunity, sadness over words spoken in anger and actions committed with hatred, regret for words of love not spoken and deeds of generosity that were considered but left undone. Each day adds to the weight of the bag, until you can hardly move it along.

In your other hand you carry your resentment and pain at all the harmful things that have been done to you, all the hurtful words thrown at you in anger or spite, all the hostile actions committed by others, words and gestures that daily assaulted and wounded you, damaging your soul and distorting your growth. The memory of them is a torment to you, but you cannot put down the burden. Every time the attempt is made, you feel compelled to pick up the bag once more before recommencing your journey.

The day draws on; the sun becomes hotter. Sweat trickles into your eyes, and your hands blister as the handles of the bags bite into them. You can hardly move, and you close your eyes in pain and frustration. Suddenly, a shadow appears between you and the sun, blocking its harsh rays from your face. You open your eyes and a figure stands before you. He is silhouetted against the sun, so it is hard to make out his features, but you know in your heart that it is the Lord. Silently, he reaches out his hands, scarred and stained with blood. Slowly, he takes each bag from you, one by one.

In his hands the heavy bags seem to lose their substance and disappear, absorbed into the figure that looks so lovingly upon you. Freed from your burdens, you can move more lightly, and with ease you continue your journey as the landscape becomes green and fertile and the river swells and burbles once again. Then you realise that you were never alone, that the Lord has travelled by your side all the length of the route. He would willingly have shared your burdens and taken the weight of them upon himself. All you had need to do was to stop and allow him to do so. From now on, as you journey once more along the way, this is what you will be able to do.

Take some time to reflect on the action of giving to Christ the regrets and hurts that weigh you down, slowing your journey and impeding your progress. As often as you need to, hand over the burdens to Jesus and picture the freedom with which you will move in future.

Spend some time after this reflection in simply enjoying who you are, where you are right at this moment, and give thanks to God.

8   Trust yourself

ST JAMES WAY (Worcester to Bristol)

As they were going along the road, someone said to him, 'I will
follow you wherever you go.' And Jesus said to him, 'Foxes have
holes, and birds of the air have nests; but the Son of Man has
nowhere to lay his head.' To another he said, 'Follow me.' But
he said, 'Lord, first let me go and bury my father.' But Jesus said
to him, 'Let the dead bury their own dead; but as for you, go
and proclaim the kingdom of God.' Another said, 'I will follow
you, Lord; but let me first say farewell to those at my home.'
Jesus said to him, 'No one who puts a hand to the plough and
looks back is fit for the kingdom of God.'

LUKE 9:57–62

Therefore, since we are surrounded by so great a cloud of
witnesses, let us also lay aside every weight and the sin that
clings so closely, and let us run with perseverance the race that
is set before us, looking to Jesus the pioneer and perfecter of
our faith, who for the sake of the joy that was set before him
endured the cross, disregarding its shame, and has taken his
seat at the right hand of the throne of God…

Endure trials for the sake of discipline. God is treating
you as children; for what child is there whom a parent does
not discipline? If you do not have that discipline in which all
children share, then you are illegitimate and not his children.
Moreover, we had human parents to discipline us, and we
respected them. Should we not be even more willing to be
subject to the Father of spirits and live? For they disciplined
us for a short time as seemed best to them, but he disciplines
us for our good, in order that we may share his holiness. Now,

discipline always seems painful rather than pleasant at the time, but later it yields the peaceful fruit of righteousness to those who have been trained by it.

Therefore lift your drooping hands and strengthen your weak knees, and make straight paths for your feet, so that what is lame may not be put out of joint, but rather be healed.

HEBREWS 12:1–2, 7–13

As part of my work, I give lectures and hold workshops on various aspects of pilgrimage. I am called upon to lecture on the history of pilgrimage, to explore its spirituality and to help groups and families discover how to make pilgrimage, either within their own neighbourhood or further afield. One such workshop, which I am regularly called upon to deliver, provides practical information about the actual way to make a pilgrimage. We discuss how to choose a route, what guidebooks to use, when to travel and with whom, what to pack, where to stay and what to expect on the journey. It is a highly practical session, designed to help the aspiring pilgrim to prepare for their journey.

The workshops themselves are interesting events, with the usual variety of people made even more diverse by the different stages they are at in their thinking about pilgrimage. First, there are those who have already made a pilgrimage. Confident and knowledgeable, they sit relaxed in their chairs, legs stretched out in front of them, hands clasped behind the backs of their heads. Occasionally they raise a quizzical eyebrow at a statement I have made, or make a face when I mention a gadget I have found useful or a book that has helped me. Their body language is superior and faintly aggressive; sometimes they cannot wait until the designated question time before they interject with comments, and often criticism, of their own.

I am not sure why these people attend such events. Surely, once a pilgrimage has been made, the necessity to find out what to pack in your rucksack or how to choose a guidebook is less urgent. Sometimes they are there to exchange information about the latest kit or to discover more about a particular route that interests them, which they have not yet attempted. Often, however, I think they are there because they are still filled with enthusiasm from their experience. They have exhausted their potential audiences at home and are seeking new forums in which to hold conversations about the incidents and adventures of the road. This group can be useful in a workshop. They can add information and share technical and navigational knowledge— as long as they don't insist that only their way of doing things or their particular pieces of kit are best for everyone.

The second type of people who attend this sort of workshop are those who are in the middle of their preparations; they may already have chosen their route, perhaps even picked their journey companions and booked their travel. These people are the most enthusiastic. Leaning forward eagerly in their chairs, notebooks at the ready, they listen carefully, anxious to extract as much useful information as they can. They ask piercing questions about the exact ideal ratio between body weight and pack weight; they debate the merits of Goretex and leather boots and have ever more technical queries over the contents of a first aid kit. They are energetic and lively. They have often begun their training and look as if they want nothing more than to tie on their boots and set off straight away, sticks in hand. (Is that one stick or two? Or none at all?)

Finally, there is a third type of people who attend these pilgrimage preparation events. They are often to be found in the back row, near the door, as if they are not sure whether they even want to be there at all. These are the people who think they might want to go on pilgrimage but are still not sure. In their heads, they are quite enthusiastic and will often attend more than one event, as if trying to workshop themselves into a state of readiness. However, there is always something—some issue or person, some concern or impending event—that prevents them from ever setting off. It is from this group of people that I get the most anxious questions. What about route finding? What about accidents or injury? How safe is it to travel alone? What are the possibilities of being attacked on the route? Do I have any statistics on the matter, or is my information all subjective?

My sympathy is always awakened by this timid, fearful group. They ask for so much encouragement and support and, yet, ultimately, it is often not external circumstances that prevent them from taking the decision finally to embark on a pilgrimage. Much that is offered by way of excuse is not entirely valid. It is normally something to hide behind, to disguise the real reason—which is often simply fear. It is a big decision to make. Training is needed; equipment must be bought, routes considered and, finally, courage gathered to set off from all that is familiar, to risk the unknown and be prepared to face every eventuality, relying only on their own strength and courage to take them through.

We are right to be anxious, even fearful, for a long-distance pilgrimage can be a significant event in our lives, challenging us mentally, emotionally and physically. It has always been recognised as such, from the earliest times, when to embark on a pilgrimage to Santiago de Compostela or Rome was truly to risk one's life, never mind a journey as fraught with danger as one with Jerusalem as the destination.

In medieval times, the serious business of undertaking a pilgrimage was highlighted by the number of tasks that pilgrims had to perform before they were allowed to set off. Permission had to be obtained from the local priest—and the landowner as well, if the aspiring pilgrim was under a feudal obligation. All debts had to be cleared and a will had to be drawn up, as there was a good chance that the pilgrim would not return, so great were the perils to be encountered. A *testimoniales*—a document certifying the genuine nature of the journey—would provide some measure of safety and occasional free food and lodging, but it was not total proof of safety from attack by the marauding bands who haunted the main merchant route across Britain and the Continent. At a final service held in the church, the uniform of staff, cloak, hat and bag were blessed in the hope of obtaining spiritual protection before the pilgrim could set off on his journey.

This uniform would become well known throughout Europe as the sign of the pilgrim, often augmented by a badge signifying the hoped-for destination—a scallop shell for Santiago de Compostela, the crossed keys of St Peter for Rome, and palm leaves for Jerusalem. The badge would offer protection and courage, enabling the wearer to draw strength from his knowledge of the many thousands of pilgrims who had walked the same route.

There is evidence of the great importance attached to the dress of the pilgrim and its symbolic significance for the wearer, in the very place where one popular pilgrim route begins. Worcester Cathedral was a popular pilgrimage destination for those who wished to ask for healing at the shrine of St Wulfstan, Bishop of Worcester from 1062 until 1095. He was an early campaigner against the slave trade, having great concern for the poor and dispossessed of his county. He restored many churches in the area, building Great Malvern Priory and rebuilding much of Worcester Cathedral itself.

In the heart of this majestic building, in 1986, a body was discovered, buried near one of the pillars in the nave of the cathedral. The skeleton, whose skull was missing, probably as the result of earlier excavations, was wearing long boots, worn down with travel. There was also buried with him a hat bearing a cockleshell badge made of horn, and a long staff. These are believed to be the remains of Robert Sutton, a citizen of Worcester. Analysis of his skeleton revealed a man who had probably made more than one long journey or pilgrimage. A life of arduous walks had left him with severe arthritis in his legs, toes, spine, ribs and pelvis. As well as causing him 'considerable pain', it had led to fusion of some bones of the spine, coccyx, ribs and sternum, which would have had a crippling effect.

The stocky, thick-set pilgrim must have led an adventurous life: his skeleton bears the scars of two arrowheads on his left thigh. He survived the attack, to die in his 60s, but it left him permanently disabled and in pain. Still, this did not prevent him from being so affected by his experiences that he clearly expressed a wish to be buried in his pilgrim's outfit—a reminder both of his physical journey and, perhaps, of his spiritual place as a pilgrim and sojourner in the world. What better place to begin a journey from the heartland of England, following the

Severn, the UK's longest river, to the ancient port of Bristol, where ships would have set off for the lengthy and risky journey to the countries of the Mediterranean and beyond?

The route along the River Severn from Worcester to Bristol is better known as the Severn Way, but would undoubtedly have been used by pilgrims as well as merchants and other travellers as they made the first stage of their journey to the Continent. Following the course of the river as it meanders through the English countryside, the route also passes through some beautiful historic towns, developed from settlements springing up on the fertile banks of the wide river, offering both transport links and water power to local economies. Tewkesbury and Gloucester afford an opportunity to view hundreds of years of architecture in the mixed buildings that have grown up by the water edge as Bristol is approached along the Severn Beach.

This is a peaceful, easy route, not demanding great feats of endurance in terms of steep tracks or barren plains, with plenty of prosperous towns and villages along the route to provide food and accommodation. The route is practically impassable at certain times of year, however, when the effects of flooding make the riverside paths unnavigable. Once the winter storms are over, the path follows—like the river—the path of least resistance at the bottom of the valleys, alongside green water meadows and shady woods. Certainly this route could be described as ideal for those whose anxieties about embarking on a pilgrimage are mainly to do with the physical effort required.

This is not to deny that any pilgrimage requires a degree of physical robustness and an acceptance of a certain amount of pain. Although most people can walk anything up to ten miles during the length of one day, the challenge of a long-distance journey is that of rising again the next day, and the next, and repeating the effort. Legs that are unused to sustained physical exertion will quickly begin to ache, and any weaknesses in the joints or bones will rapidly make themselves apparent. Support bandages and cold compresses can help, but I have seen many weary walkers in tears as they faced another day of pain—tears wept both at the prospect of hours of agony and at the alternative thought of having to end a journey so long in the planning and preparation, holder of so many hopes and aspirations.

Even if these difficulties can be avoided by steady and gradually increasing days of training beforehand, strange buzzing feelings in toes and heels that herald a developing blister, along with all the soreness and misery that toes bring with them, are a hazard that almost no walker can avoid. However hardened the traveller, a day's journey in the rain, with miles of walking in wet socks and boots, can provoke a blister on almost any foot, added to the strength-sapping necessity of marching in gradually dampening clothes, visibility limited by the water cascading from the hood of a raincoat.

These days of aching limbs, sore feet and wet bodies, however, lose all power to alarm and despond the moment the sun breaks through and the pilgrim is able once more to look up and view the glorious countryside as it unfolds before them at a pace slow enough for all the variety and wealth of colour and texture to be truly appreciated. Then, we can rejoice in the gift of physical movement that is ours, despite the cost of sore muscles, enabling us to be part of the landscape in a way that gives a precious and unique insight into the work of its Creator. Then, we rejoice at the courage that made us determine to take the first step along the route, and the perseverance that enabled us to continue even when the challenges increased.

A similar degree of courage and endurance can be called for, to manage our spiritual journey, not only while on a pilgrimage but also on our return home. There are inevitably times when what is asked of us seems to be more than we can give, when our burdens are greater than we can easily bear, and when the desire to stop and give up seems overwhelming. Sometimes these burdens and fears will stem from past hurts or future anxieties, burdens that can be acknowledged and set aside (see Chapter 7). At other times, however, the way may take us through the very darkest of valleys, until it seems as if the shadows of death surround us and those we love, threatening to overwhelm us. At such times, consolation is very difficult to come by and the comforting words of others can seem trite and empty in the face of the suffering we are enduring. Perhaps then our help may come from the knowledge of all those who have endured before us, remaining faithful to God in the dark times, emerging finally into the light, aware that his love was with them all the time, even when they were not aware of it.

Remember Joseph, who spent at least two years imprisoned by Potiphar, having been sold into slavery by his brothers. Consider Daniel, jailed for refusing to bow down to the king, and David, who spent much time in hiding from King Saul's jealousy. Nor did the New Testament characters, tasked with sharing the good news of Jesus' love for all people, escape stonings, beatings, imprisonment, torture or death—punishments meted out to Christians from the very beginning and still continuing today. Perhaps, all we can do is kneel silently with these long-dead heroes and saints, and pray the words scratched upon a concentration camp wall by a World War II prisoner:

I believe in the sun
even when it is not shining.
And I believe in love
even when there is no one there.
And I believe in God
even when he is silent.

Reflection

In the middle of the Old Testament, just after the story of Job, comes a set of 150 poems—laments, liturgies, complaints and hymns—which make up the book of Psalms. Within these sets of verse—ranging in length from the two verses of Psalm 117, calling us to 'praise the Lord', to Psalm 119, whose 176 verses express the writer's relationship with God's commandments—almost every experience and emotion can be found. It is in the psalms that we find words to praise God for his goodness to us and for his wonderful care for each one of us: 'I will give to the Lord the thanks due to his righteousness, and sing praise to the name of the Lord, the Most High' (Psalm 7:17). We can use the psalms to encourage each other to faith and praise: 'Sing praises to the Lord, O you his faithful ones, and give thanks to his holy name' (30:4). In many of the psalms, we read of rejoicing in God's love and for the way he has rescued the psalmist from dangers and foes: 'I will extol you, O Lord, for you have drawn me up, and did not let my foes rejoice over me' (30:1).

However, it would be entirely wrong to think that the book of Psalms contains only words of joyfulness and optimism. Although many of them do ring out with triumphant praise, often this is an expression of victory after suffering, rejoicing after times of darkness. If we are looking for ways to tell God of our sufferings, to complain at the way we have been treated or to lament over our misfortunes, it is to the psalms once more that we can turn. Psalm 88 lists the difficulties that the writer is suffering: he has a soul full of troubles (v. 3) and wonders what he has done wrong, to be treated in this way: 'O Lord, why do you cast me off? Why do you hide your face from me?' (v. 14). Within the psalms, too, we find the sense of undeserved punishment and bewilderment with which we face some disasters: 'The mighty stir up strife against me. For no transgression or sin of mine, O Lord, for no fault of mine, they run and make ready' (59:3–4).

When we need to lift our voices in pain to our Creator God, we are given the words to do so, knowing that as we suffer, so have others in the past and so will others in the future until the world is completely redeemed and God's kingdom comes on earth. For beneath the anger, the lack of comprehension, the sorrow and the pain in the voices of the psalmists runs a steadfast belief in the loving goodness of God. Time and again we hear of sorrow at misfortune, which, even as it is expressed, segues imperceptibly into a reminder of God's loving faithfulness. So, Psalm 6 begins in anguish with 'You, O Lord—how long?' (v. 3) but moves into a determined belief that God will not only attend to the writer's cry but has indeed already heard it: 'The Lord has heard my supplication' (v. 9). 'Happy is everyone who trusts in you' (84:12), even when all seems dark. In fact, the psalms seem to assert that the best time to praise God is when we are in the depths of despair, for it is only when we turn to him and call upon him, when we recognise our dependence upon him, that we truly find him.

A very wise man once told me that a daily reading of the psalms is like water dripping on a stone. We initially notice no change, but gradually, imperceptibly, the rock is shaped by the water dripping, one drop at a time, on to the solid surface. So, too, will we be changed over time by our patient reading of the psalms—a small number of verses a day, read regularly and prayerfully. We will see the effects of the psalmists' careful instruction as it shapes us into the person God wants us to be.

Praise the Lord!
Praise God in his sanctuary;
    praise him in his mighty firmament!
Praise him for his mighty deeds;
    praise him according to his surpassing greatness!
Praise him with trumpet sound;
    praise him with lute and harp!
Praise him with tambourine and dance;
    praise him with strings and pipe!
Praise him with clanging cymbals;
    praise him with loud clashing cymbals!
Let everything that breathes praise the Lord!
Praise the Lord!
PSALM 150

9 Respect the community

THAMES PILGRIM WAY (Oxford to Binsey)

After this the Lord appointed seventy others and sent them on ahead of him in pairs to every town and place where he himself intended to go. He said to them, 'The harvest is plentiful, but the labourers are few; therefore ask the Lord of the harvest to send out labourers into his harvest. Go on your way. See, I am sending you out like lambs into the midst of wolves. Carry no purse, no bag, no sandals; and greet no one on the road. Whatever house you enter, first say, "Peace to this house!" And if anyone is there who shares in peace, your peace will rest on that person; but if not, it will return to you. Remain in the same house, eating and drinking whatever they provide, for the labourer deserves to be paid. Do not move about from house to house. Whenever you enter a town and its people welcome you, eat what is set before you; cure the sick who are there, and say to them, "The kingdom of God has come near to you."'

LUKE 10:1–9

One of the most joyous experiences of a pilgrimage can be the encounter between the one who travels and the one who offers hospitality and rest. The hostels along the main Camino de Santiago de Compostela are, for the most part, staffed by volunteers, people who give up some months, years or even the greater part of their lives to provide food and lodging to those who are making the long and arduous journey through the Spanish countryside. These dedicated men and women offer not just physical nourishment and rest, but also encouragement and support, information and advice to those who travel. Most of the pilgrims who receive this hospitality are deeply grateful, aware of the sacrifices that are being made for them. Only a few treat the generosity of their hosts as their due, their arrogance disturbing the harmony of the community and threatening the tradition of hospitality graciously given and received. Just as a piece of litter dropped carelessly in the middle of a forest mars the landscape that surrounds it, so an assumption of privilege can alter the peaceful coexistence of traveller and host. It is the duty of each pilgrim to treat with respect and gratitude all that is offered to them along the way, and to offer politeness and thankfulness in return.

The Thames Pilgrim's Way stretches for 100 miles, from Radcot Bridge, Oxfordshire in the east to Wraysbury, Berkshire in the west. It follows the route of the Thames Path, but it is more than that. Through the initiative of Rt Revd John Pritchard while he was Bishop of Oxford, the path that follows the River Thames as it flows through the Diocese of Oxford has been given a spiritual dimension, one that enables pilgrims to reflect on different aspects of their spiritual as well as their physical journey.

The Way begins in the remoter regions of west Oxfordshire, where the Thames is only just navigable and settlements are small and infrequent. For many miles the pilgrim may not see any sign of human life or habitation, kept company solely by the cattle grazing at the water's edge and by the rich and varied birdlife that frequent the area. Gradually, the places bordering the river become more populous; bridges begin to carry traffic across the water, and small villages can be seen nearby.

The path leads through Wolvercote on the outskirts of Oxford, before accompanying the Thames (renamed the Isis for this section) through the city itself, offering a glimpse from its banks of the magnificent buildings of Oxford University. Just before the dense building and business of the city itself, however, the river borders Port Meadow, an ancient meadow which has not known the plough in over 4000 years. The meadow stretches out on the north bank, grazed by placid cattle that remain undisturbed by the frantic efforts of runners and rowers or the sounds of children and dogs being called for as they escape the traces that normally hold them so closely.

Just before the Pilgrim's Way crosses the river to touch briefly the ancient meadow, a simple gravelled path leads to the right. Unsigned and uninformative, it gives no indication of where it leads, although a small cluster of houses can be seen in the distance, perhaps offering a clue to the destination of the path. Unprepossessing as it appears, however, to the pilgrim who chooses to step aside for a few hours and follow this path to its conclusion a rare gift is given—a hidden treasure set apart for the delight of those who are prepared to seek it.

The path leads initially to the village of Binsey, a small cluster of 17th- and 18th-century cottages, now mostly owned by Christ Church, one of the colleges of the University of Oxford. Well kept and self-consciously charming, they are gathered around a small green, at one corner of which can be found the Perch tavern, at another the road leading from the busy Botley Road into Oxford, and, at the furthermost edge, a small track winding away from village, river and city. Following this track, the pilgrim is plunged into deep countryside, with only the hum of traffic from the bypass reminding the walker that other people exist at all. At the end of the track, now lined with sycamore trees, a small iron gate leads past a pen of goats and through a copse, then opening out into a small churchyard, at the end of which nestles a simple church.

The church itself is dedicated to St Margaret of Antioch, but the nearby well is associated with St Frideswide, a Saxon saint—perhaps an indication of two different Christian communities trying to draw together in the local operation of their faith. According to legend, St Frideswide was the daughter of Didan and Sefrida, the king and queen of Oxford. Didan founded a monastery where Frideswide wished to live, this being a typical event of Saxon times, with religious houses ruled by royal leaders. The villainous Algar, king of Leicester, fell in love with Frideswide and sent men to plead his suit. Upon her refusal, they tried to kidnap her, but 'as the holy virgin spoke, their eyes were struck blind'. On repenting of their deeds they were healed, and returned to Algar, who, undeterred by their tales of sudden blindness, set out in person, 'mad with rage and fury' to capture the princess.

Frideswide, however, was warned of his approach by an angel and she escaped to Bampton, where she remained for three years, working many miracles.

On their eventual return to Oxford, Frideswide and her companions decided to pause at Binsey for a period of retreat. Finding an isolated rural place called Thornbury, they built an oratory and obtained 'by prayer' a well. Frideswide's monastic life continued at Oxford, as did the miracles that occurred even on the occasion of her funeral.

With the legendary elements extracted, the facts of St Frideswide's life do imply that, as abbess of Oxford priory, the settlement at Thornbury (or Binsey as it became known) was used by her as a place of retreat until her death in 727.

It is not necessary for travellers to know this; nor is it vital that they descend the steps to the well that lies to the west of the church. A small, narrow set of stairs leads to a dark hole, at the bottom of which can be seen the somewhat menacing dark waters, endowed with healing properties by Frideswide herself and a site of pilgrimage for those seeking healing from eye complaints. It is not even necessary to pick up the simple leaflet detailing the historic and architectural features of the church: the original Saxon building has disappeared, and only the Norman chancel and font escaped remodelling in the 13th century; 15th-century windows remain, and furniture dating from a vigorous Victorian restoration. All that is required is to enter this still, holy place and rest for a while, absorbing the atmosphere of peace and prayer that pervade the small building, its simple whitewashed walls providing a protective space within which the mind might wander and reflect, seek and perhaps find healing and transformation.

After a while, when the urge to move on makes itself known, the pilgrim may be drawn to the greatest treasure contained by this unassuming building. Lying almost unnoticed on top of a bookcase by the entrance is a modest book with a pen nearby. It is here that the thoughts and impressions of those visiting this place are recorded and shared with the people who come after them. In here can be found a record of those who have been before, and the ways in which their lives have been touched and changed by their visit. Some of the comments are simple and factual—a name and an address, for example, simply recording the fact that a visitor has occupied the space for a short while before moving on. These entries might seem to reveal very little, but still they demonstrate a willingness to be counted, as it were, a willingness to become part of the community of visitors to Binsey, in however slight or brief a way.

Other comments appear to be offering a justification for a visit—a connection to the place which means that the visitor merits inclusion. Some of these are by virtue of ancestral links: 'My gt-gt-gt-grandfather buried here'; 'My family married here in the mid-19th century'. Others reflect more personal connections: 'Married here in 1969'; 'Just 50 years ago we were married here in this church.' For some visitors, frequency of visit appears to bring with it a kind of status, the visit being a reason in itself: 'I return yet again to this place.' These visitors seem to seek something that only the peace of Binsey can offer: 'Again here, again good, and again thank goodness it's open.' A sense of welcome and belonging is shared by many who choose to record their impressions in the book: 'Visited today and was welcomed warmly by the beauty of the church.' Some of the entries are conversational, imparting information or recording their knowledge of the history of the church and its associations: 'Very interesting to learn of the connection with Lewis Carroll's Alice'; 'I do believe in God and especially after reading "The Twilight of Atheism".' The church is addressed as if it were a sentient being ('Beloved Binsey') and many writers show a willingness to engage in conversation with the rest of the community of the book. 'Binsey feels a bit neglected; would you not offer a few flowers?' enquires one writer, to which the answer is written: 'Left in peace for now, not neglected, and the flowers are waiting for spring.'

However, the most moving are those that share visitors' feelings and prayers with the readers of the book—people whom they might never meet but with whom they have a connection through the place of

Binsey: 'This evening we visited the church with our newborn daughter. During the long years of longing for a child, I often visited this church for solace. With thanks for answered prayers.' Even more poignantly, they may ask these strangers for their prayers, to add to their own: 'Please pray for my sister; she's very sick'; 'Please pray for me as I take my exams.'

For the writers in this book, it seems as if it is not about the journey, after all. Over the years, hundreds of people have made their way along the narrow tree-lined track to this small, insignificant church, intending to seek the peace and space for reflection that can be found there, and to offer and ask for prayer. Returning to the medieval emphasis which always lay with the destination rather than the route leading to that place, these pilgrims make the journey, however short, to add their names to the lists of others who have watched and waited in the holy place. They do so knowing that they are not alone, that their feelings and prayers have been shared by others, some of whom have written them down, while the heartfelt longings and rejoicings of others are held in the fabric of the building itself.

It is a strange community, this—one which finds its centre in a worn, slightly damp notebook in a tiny rural church. Yet it is no stranger than the one that gradually built up around the young man with the unfathomable eyes and radical way of speech who emerged from the wilderness to be baptised by John in the River Jordan. From that first invitation to two fishermen by the shores of Lake Galilee, to the invitation he extends to each one of us, he calls us to become part of that huge community of Christian people that covers every part of the world, from the largest cathedral congregations to the smallest gathering of two or three in prayer. We are asked by Jesus himself to shed our selfishness, our grasping need to possess, our yearning for status and power, and to join him in humility and love, sharing our knowledge and wealth, our comfort and stability with those who require these things, offering generously from our store, knowing that we in return will receive those things which we most need.

It is within this community of fellow travellers along the Way that we will find our longing for a true home at least partially satisfied—a longing for a home that is only dimly remembered or maybe never at all experienced. Just as the visitors to Binsey find the sensations of home in that small, isolated building ('Couldn't get home so came here; a wonderful substitute'), so we may discover it in our own church or among our fellow believers, mindful always that our true home will only be discovered at the end of the journey.

It is through living with, praying for and working among those with whom we share our Christian journey that we will find the company we need if we are to grow and develop in our knowledge and love of the one who first invited us to make the journey. The visitors to Binsey church do not hesitate to bring others with them, to experience the special atmosphere of the place ('Brought a friend to meet a friend') or to celebrate events and occasions: 'The stag crew'; 'I finished my exams. I came here again with my friend.'

Stories of some of these visitors can be traced throughout the books. 'What a beautiful day! Today here in this church, X said she will marry me!' is followed, further on in the book, by the entry 'A year ago we got engaged, standing right here—what a wonderful place to have started our lives together.' So, too, a regular faithful gathering in community to pray and share together will build up a record of God's saving and redemptive actions, enabling the members of that community to look back upon their joint history and see the hand of God at work in all that they have experienced.

The community at Binsey, held within the visitors' book, protected by the sturdy walls of the surrounding building, is a safe place to bring troubles and fears. Some find peace and hope through visiting the church and stopping for a while: 'So peaceful and set apart from a busy world.' Just as Jesus stepped aside so many times during his ministry, to reflect and pray, so we are led to do the same, either on our own or with others. It is through these times of shared prayer that understanding can grow and deepen—our understanding of ourselves and of each other and of God, who underpins our lives and shares his love with all who ask for it. As Jesus taught his disciples how to pray, so we can learn from him and from others how to offer everything in our lives to God in prayer.

This is not to declare that living in a Christian community, however loosely defined this community is, will not be without its troubles or stresses. It is incredibly hard to share our lives with others, to put the needs of others before our own needs, or even before our desires. Inevitably, there will be times of stress and strain. For the pilgrims to Binsey, stress came with the felling of the avenue of chestnut trees that sheltered the way to the church. Although they were diseased, the loss of these trees caused anger and upset among the writers in the book: 'What the heck have all those trees been cut down for!!! That was a beautiful lane leading up to the church! Complete human insensitivity!!! Very angry.' The effects of the loss are clearly not just upon the beauty of the place, but upon its spirit as well, and the capacity for healing that belongs to Binsey is seen to be in some way damaged: 'The avenue of trees was part of the church and holy well and was integral in making this a special place.' Some people compare the loss of the trees to their own spiritual distress: 'Seeking peace from one tragic loss, I am confronted by the loss of the trees.' However, even as events in Binsey cause distress, so too can they provide healing, as other writers in the book offer consolation: 'The chestnuts lived their life. It was time for them to go and new trees will be planted, then they too will grow (God willing).'

By contributing to the book, by writing an entry in it, visitors become part of the community of Binsey. They find within the book the validation and recognition of their feelings about the place and about its spiritual importance in their lives. It provides a place not only where the story of Binsey can be told but where it can be added to.

So, too, with us and our own communities of family, friends, neighbours and churches. These communities, particularly the ones centred around our churches or worshipping congregations, may seem to be fractured and dysfunctional. It may appear that they bring little that is good and much that is harmful to our lives. It may seem easier simply to seek solitude and isolation. But, although there will always be occasions when withdrawal from the crowd to reflect and pray is essential and helpful, this way of life is not the one for which we were designed by God. From the first days, when Eve was created as a companion for Adam, the children of God have lived in community. These communities have been small or large, thriving or barely surviving, but never alone. Jesus himself gathered twelve people around him to support him in his journey and to be taught by him in return. The disciples were sent out not alone but in groups or pairs to share the gospel with the people they met. And we are told that 'where two or three are gathered in my name, I am there among them' (Matthew 18:20).

God wants us to live in community, to share the good news of his love with others and to work together to bring his kingdom nearer. This will not be an easy task; it will require patience, forbearance and unselfishness, but we will not be left to struggle alone, and the moments of joy and love that are shared will prove good compensation for the challenges and trials of living with others. We do not travel alone but in the company of many others, fellow saints throughout the world who, together with us, seek to write the story of God's salvation upon the pages of this earth. As our own individual faith journeys are lived, they become part of that greater story, adding to the glory of God and celebrating his love for his children. The places at which we pause for refreshment and reflection, the communities in which we find a temporary home, become part of our story and of God's, weaving love and peace into the everyday struggles of existence, adding a shining thread of hope to the fabric of our lives and the lives of those around us.

Reflection

The physical pilgrim, journeying a short or long distance along a pilgrimage route, will find many ways to honour the communities through which the pilgrim road leads. From simple actions such as following the walker's code of taking only photographs and leaving only footprints, to more intentional kindness such as picking up litter from along the route, the traveller can, if they so wish, even arrange to spend some time at a hostel as a member of the hospitality team, offering the kindness and generosity that they have experienced to others in their turn, enabling the usual hosts to take some time out from their usual round of duties. More intangible ways of expressing gratitude and recognition for gifts received can also be employed.

One habit which can be adopted is that of making a pledge at the beginning of any journey to pause at every church that is passed. If the church is open, it should be entered. Prayers or, better still, a short service of thanksgiving should be offered for the gift of the building and its presence within the community. Church members and the wider community can be prayed for, as well as those travellers who have gone before and those who will follow after. If candles are available, even if it is not your tradition, consider dropping the required number of coins in the wooden box and setting a candle burning as a physical sign of your invocation of blessings upon the place.

If the church is closed, as, sadly, so many churches must be in these days church fixtures and fittings are of increasing value, why not practise 'clypping' the church? This is based on an Anglo-Saxon custom, revived in the 1800s as a way of expressing fellowship and love both for the church and for the church community it holds. 'Clypping' means clasping or holding tightly. If there are enough people in your group, hold hands in a circle around the outside of the church. If you are few in number, you can simply walk round the building as you pray, pausing at each corner for a time of silence. If you have the time and resources, the Arthur Rank Centre (arthurrankcentre.org.uk) offers a model 'clypping service', which can be adapted to suit local needs. The website offers a poem by ee cummings, 'I am a little church', which describes the sense of the unhurried timelessness of a church building, and how this can point us towards God.

10 Rejoice in the journey

ST OLAV'S WAY (Stiklestad to Trondheim)

Awe came upon everyone, because many wonders and signs were being done by the apostles. All who believed were together and had all things in common; they would sell their possessions and goods and distribute the proceeds to all, as any had need. Day by day, as they spent much time together in the temple, they broke bread at home and ate their food with glad and generous hearts, praising God and having the goodwill of all the people. And day by day the Lord added to their number those who were being saved.

ACTS 2:43–47

The lecture room was filled to capacity: row after row of functional folding chairs were filled with mostly older people, although here and there a few who seemed to be in their early 20s stood about amid the greying audience. The chairman cleared his throat and introduced the speakers for the evening—a straight-faced couple in their early 60s who had celebrated the onset of their retirement by walking from Roncesvalles on the borders of Spain and France, along the Camino Frances to Santiago de Compostela.

They had done it the correct way, they informed us earnestly—taking all that they needed in rucksacks, which they had diligently carried every step by themselves. They had stayed only at pilgrim hostels, leaving early to benefit from the cool morning air and arriving in good time to secure the best-situated beds. They had followed the advice of the guide books, taking their boots off at every break, stopping at hourly intervals to rehydrate and resting for at least 20 minutes every two hours, eating high-energy snacks before continuing along the marked path. Regular churchgoers, they had begun and ended each day with a simple service and had stopped at all the churches and sites of historical interest on the way. They had suffered a bit from blisters and one member of the party had had trouble with his knees, but, on the whole, the party had remained physically fit, mostly due to the training they had undertaken before setting off.

The entire trip had been well planned, well organised and efficiently executed. Yet, as I watched and listened, I felt strangely uneasy. The sense of something lacking was clarified for me by a remark overheard on the way out: a man turned to his companion and muttered under his breath, 'Doesn't sound like much bloody fun, does it?' This comment captured the essence of the pilgrimage as it was reported to me in that hall—not much fun. For some, pilgrimage is indeed an intensely serious business, approached with caution and undertaken with apprehensions, so laden down is it with expectation.

For a pilgrim of this nature, dedicated and serious, the 139 kilometres from Stiklestad to Nideros might seem ideal. St Olav's Way celebrates the conversion of Norway to Christianity by Olav Haroldsohn, first king of Norway. Born in 995, this Viking was converted to Christianity while fighting in Europe; he was baptised in Rouen and returned to Norway with the aim of converting the country to Christianity, unifying it in the process. He met fierce opposition from many of the local chieftains but, none the less, achieved his goal to become the first king over the whole of Norway. He was ousted by Cnut in 1028 and spent time in exile before returning again in 1030, landing at Selangor. His attempt to regain the throne was unsuccessful, and he was killed in July 1030 at Stiklestad. His body was taken by supporters and buried on the banks of the River Nid.

Rumours of healings and miracles taking place at this site developed and the magnificent cathedral built to house his tomb at Nidaros (modern-day Trondheim) was finally completed in 1300. In its heyday, before the Black Death devastated the country in 1349 and made travel impossible, Nidaros was the fourth most popular pilgrimage, after

Rome, Jerusalem and Santiago. As with other long-distance pilgrim routes, a network of hostels and shelters developed for the travellers, as well as the wonderful Olav fields—special fields, five or six miles apart, designated for the rest and pasturage of pilgrim horses. The Reformation in the 16th century ended this route, as it did so many others, destroying the abbeys that provided shelter, as well as the shrine of Olav itself.

During the 1990s, the route was revived and would seem to be a good choice indeed for those who take their challenges—and their pilgrimages—seriously. The route is not easy. The hills can become mountains, bringing with them the changeable mountain weather. Navigation is not for the beginner: although the path is marked with signs, they are not quite close enough to follow without the help of a map, and the route is not walked often enough for a clear pathway to be evident. There is accommodation along the route but it can be at quite lengthy intervals and there is no alternative if disaster strikes. It is expensive too, as is the cost of food and drink, which in places has to be carried in sufficient quantities to last two or three days, as there is a lack of supporting infrastructure.

This can all sound quite disheartening, but it is, in fact, only realistic. Pilgrimage in Norway is a serious business and should not be undertaken lightly. The infrastructure is still too thin to allow much reliance on the goodwill of others to rescue a situation. But to approach a pilgrimage in an overly serious state of mind, weighed down with expectations of emotional and spiritual outcome, can be self-defeating. If the adventure is too burdened, how can it take wings and fly? If it is too hemmed in with structure and targets, where will space be found for the unexpected, the transformative?

Better, perhaps, to sit more lightly to the task of pilgrimage and seek the joy that is to be found on the journey, wherever it arises. So we learn not to see the dark woods of the Norwegian hillsides, silent and intense, dim light filtering though the densely packed trees, but to exclaim with joy at the shaft of light in the clearing, shining on the tiny frail pine saplings as they reach towards the sky. Instead of bemoaning the exorbitant cost of food and shelter, we can enjoy the benefits of living simply—of really tasting the plain fare, sustaining and wholesome. Instead of trying to foresee every eventuality, we can enter into the spirit of adventure that inhabits a path so infrequently walked: only 176 people walked the 100 kilometres necessary to gain the 'St Olav Diploma' at the Nidaros Pilgrim Centre in Trondheim in 2015.

Over the years, my memories of pilgrimage stand out like photographs: groups of weary pilgrims squealing with cold as they bathe their hot, aching feet in an icy mountain stream; my young children rolling down a grassy hillside, laughing and dizzy; a husband tenderly bathing his wife's blistered feet; the look of concentration on a young man's face as he discusses the future of Christianity with his companion. I remember the shouts of joy as a hill is crested and the hostel is spotted nestling at the bottom of the slope; the taste of rough red wine in the evening and the way it loosens tongues silenced by fatigue; the sight of rolling hills spreading far into the distance, stamped with the bright stone of the pilgrim route.

Pilgrimage is companionship at a level deeper than we usually experience, pain sharper than we may have previously suffered, and joy richer than ever anticipated. It is a path, a discovering, a process.

The best gift we can receive from the road is that of celebrating each step of life's journey. Sometimes the way will be hard; the route may become obscured; pain and suffering may slow us down. At other times, green hills and loving companionship will make many miles seem but a few feet, filled with rejoicing. We offer a heart full of praise, prepared to accept the dangers and delights of the journey, open to every day's adventure. In return we receive the assurance of a constant travelling companion who not only walks alongside us but comes to meet us as we approach our journey's end, ready to embrace us and lead us home.

Reflection

Either on the internet or in a book, find a copy of Rublev's icon of the Trinity. Pictures mounted on to wooden boards can often be found in religious bookshops or church gift shops. Find a place where you can sit in comfort, where you will not be disturbed and where you can focus easily. Place the picture where it can easily be seen, ideally level with your eyes, so that you can look at it for quite a long time without needing to change your position.

Rublev painted this icon in 1410 and it represents the meeting of Abraham and the angels in Genesis 18, where three strangers are entertained by him under an oak tree at Mamre. They later prophesy the birth of Sarah's child, Isaac. The icon is also said to represent the Trinity as the Father, Son and Holy Spirit gather round the Communion table, making the shape of a chalice as they do.

Spend some time in silence and stillness, simply looking at the picture, and imagine yourself approaching the table. Reflect on the journey that has led you here. How has it been? What have been the times of rejoicing? Which parts have filled you with sorrow? Allow yourself to leave all behind you as you draw nearer.

Let your eyes focus on different areas of the picture. Can you see the figure looking out from the tower? Is he looking for you or is he looking with you for one or more people you have lost? Say the names of these people out loud as a blessing.

Picture yourself resting beneath the tree. You lean against its trunk, your back feeling the roughness of the bark as the sturdy tree supports you. What times or places of rest and reflection have been given you in your life? Is there such a place available to you now?

Notice how the shape of the table is that of a chalice. What has been your relationship with the church, both as an institution and as a group of people? Have there been times when you have been hurt by the church? Will you allow yourself to let go of that hurt? When have you been supported by the church, by your fellow believers? Have you offered thanks for these times?

See how the picture is filled with glowing colours of gold and green and blue—the colours of the sun, the earth and the sky. All of God's creation is in the picture. Have you made time to rejoice in what you see of God's love in the world around you? How might you do so? See the encircling gestures of the three figures, how they point to each other, offering support and unity. Are there people in your life who support you? How can you offer support in your turn?

Finally, draw your attention back to the space at the table. See the look of love in the eyes of the figures as they invite you to sit and eat with them, completing the circle. It is not time for you to join them yet, but let the knowledge that the place is prepared for you fill you with peace and joy: 'And if I go and prepare a place for you, I will come again and will take you to myself, so that where I am, there you may be also' (John 14:3).

A practical guide

This chapter is not an exhaustive list of the things you need to do before you begin a pilgrimage or of the things you should pack for your journey. It is simply a reflection on the way to travel and some notes on kit, which I am passing on to you in the hope that they will prove useful.

One of the most important things to remember when undertaking a pilgrimage is that it is your journey. You must use the time you have available to explore the places you want to travel to, both physically and spiritually. Do not allow yourself to be pressured into taking routes or using methods that are unsuitable for you, either in terms of time and money or of the way you choose to travel. The advice in this chapter is merely an offering of things you might wish to take into consideration when planning your journey and preparing yourself for the effort involved.

Before even considering such a big investment in physical and spiritual energy, it is worth spending some time simply reflecting on your reasons for undertaking such a task. A pilgrimage, especially one made on foot over a period of days, if not weeks, is a major commitment, which you should not feel pressured into simply because it appears to be the fashionable thing to do. Nor should it be regarded as a spiritual 'quick fix': the lessons learnt, although valuable, can be very hard won, and you may well need to call upon all your powers of determination and endurance before the journey is over. Make sure that you really want to put time and effort into achieving your goal, but without being overly specific about the nature of that goal. Simply getting to the end of the journey, merely arriving at the destination, is not enough. You must be open to all that the journey might offer, undertaking to receive joyfully and honestly the lessons that it will teach.

Many people have in their minds the ideal pilgrimage (see chapter 8). However, this may simply not be achievable within your own financial and time constraints, let alone with the pressures placed upon the aspiring pilgrim by work and family commitments. There is nothing wrong with making any pilgrimage in stages, in one- or two-week blocks, over a number of holidays or even years. Indeed, the sense of achievement when finally reaching the destination may be even greater due to the amount of time it took to complete the journey.

The way you travel will also affect your itinerary and route. Some pilgrimage routes can only be made by foot, while others will be open to cyclists. Still other trails can be followed in a vehicle, allowing a greater amount of terrain to be covered, although it could be argued that the effect is lessened when the pilgrim is shielded from the most dramatic effects by the ability simply to cut short the trip and escape to the nearest town or city! However, if you can only manage such an undertaking by car or coach, then do not allow this to prevent you from experiencing the effects of pilgrimage.

However long you take to make the journey and however gentle the stages in which you walk, you will still need to undertake some training if the pilgrimage is on foot. Years of walking with groups of pilgrims, and my own experience also, have taught me that almost anyone with any degree of fitness can undertake a one-day pilgrimage of some ten or twelve miles and gain enormous benefit from it. Time spent out in the open air, either in the company of others or alone in order to reflect, is an invaluable experience and well worth the sore limbs and incipient blisters that may be accompanying you by the end of the day.

However, when it comes to getting up the next morning and repeating the exercise that day and the next and the next, a different level of fitness is required. The endurance required to undertake a journey of a week or two, or even longer, should not be underestimated, and the only way to build up that endurance is by walking. Regular walking, ideally of two or three days together, can build up enough stamina so that the challenge of an unfit body is not one that has to be met and overcome on the journey. If your training walks can be undertaken wearing the same kit that will be worn while engaged on pilgrimage, this will give the opportunity of fine-tuning what to wear and what to take so that it best meets your individual needs.

When leading groups, it is worth remembering that most people overestimate their personal level of fitness, believing that they can walk far more miles than is actually the case. Useful, also, is the advice that the larger the group, the slower and more spread out it tends to get, often doubling the journey time.

The level of fitness you can realistically achieve before setting off will also dictate the type of route you choose. If you are already extremely used to long-distance walking, you can feel free to choose routes where the infrastructure is less well established, with longer gaps between hostels and fewer opportunities for rest stops. If, however, you are averagely fit, and particularly if this is your first pilgrimage, it is probably advisable to choose a well-known route, with lots of hostels and hotels as well as plenty of shops and inns to offer refreshment along the way. The Confraternity of Saint James website (www.csj.org.uk) has a good selection of routes that you can look at, as well as links to the sites dedicated to each particular route.

Some of the most popular routes, such as that to Santiago de Compostela, do not necessitate buying a map, as the route is clearly signposted all along the way, and in any case there are enough fellow pilgrims to ask if the route becomes confusing. However, a guidebook will help you make the most of the journey, and it becomes essential for some of the less well-travelled routes, where the path is not so well marked and the way itself has not been worn down by the passage of previous travellers.

It is not essential that you complete the entire length of the pilgrim route all in one go. For some routes, indeed, this would be impossible, as it takes many weeks. Sit lightly to the distance, being realistic about the number of miles you will actually cover, taking into account the fact that you might wish to stop in some of the cities and see the sights or have a meal and a rest for a couple of hours in a restaurant or hotel. Be realistic about your daily mileage: some hardy souls will travel up to 20 miles a day, others only eight. It depends greatly on the number in your party and their ability to walk. Most pilgrims walk about twelve miles a day, which is a good number to base your calculations on. The potential for a journey to become a grim trudge towards a longed-for destination, cheerlessly marking off the number of miles still to do before the experience ends, is very real and should be avoided. Better to relax and enjoy the journey, ignoring the number of people striding past you, than arrive worn out and in pain, not having benefited from the experience.

Don't forget you will need a day to travel at either end of the trip, and, if the journey ends in a famous pilgrim destination such as Santiago de Compostela, a day to spend there as well. For some, the chance to obtain a 'compostela' or the 'Olav diploma', or any one of the certificates that celebrate the journey on foot of more than 100 km along a route, can be the deciding factor in the choice of journey. This is perfectly acceptable and such trips are undertaken by many thousands of pilgrims each year, but it is worth considering whether the sense of achievement might be greater if the final 100 kilometres are approached from further afield, the journey being broken up over a number of weeks or years.

The number of people in your group will greatly affect your choice of destination, the speed at which you travel and the number of days you will take to complete your journey. Large parties walking together will walk at a slower speed and require more in the way of infrastructure. Some smaller hostels and hotels will not be able to cope with a large group at all; others may not have enough rooms free, thus forcing people into different lodgings. Finding places for food along the way may be more challenging and the stops will certainly be longer as everyone will need to order, eat and get ready to move on. However, the joys of walking alongside a wide variety of companions, sharing experiences and hearing life stories, does much to mitigate against the disadvantage of taking a large group.

If you wish to travel fast, travel alone or with just one companion: you will not need so many discussions about where best to eat or how long to rest. Some pilgrims arrive alone at a starting point, with the aim of meeting others as they travel. This is perhaps the most interesting way, as all sorts of nationalities and types will be encountered and the journey made colourful by the narratives of your companions.

However you travel, it is important to be hospitable and generous to those who share the route. A whole new system of assessing people, not based on appearance or job title, comes into being on a pilgrimage route. People are judged on their cheerfulness, their willingness to share their knowledge and possessions, and the way they help others along the route. The cost and newness of your kit will impress people much less than your willingness to offer up your last blister plaster or a clean pair of socks to those who need it!

With regard to packing, it is important to take as little as you can possibly get away with. This book does not aim to give an exhaustive list of what to take and what to leave behind; the CSJ website offers not only kit lists but an extensive forum of discussions over what has been found useful by others on the same route. There are a few principles that should be borne in mind, however. You should first decide on how much electronic equipment, if any, you are going to take with you. Almost every pilgrim takes a mobile phone with them for emergencies, but many make the decision not to use it except for weekly phone calls home, vowing to remain free of modern communication devices for the period of the journey. This not only gives more time to reflection, but offers space for recording one's thoughts and feelings in a journal rather than relying on music or reading to fill in the empty spaces of the day. It also means you will not be part of the competition to find the few available plug sockets for recharging your device on your arrival at the hostel.

Bear in mind, also, the simple calculation that the more you take, the heavier your pack will be. A heavy pack will result in greater fatigue, more likelihood of blisters and the possibility of backache and sore hips and shoulders. The anxious ones who take precautions against every possible accident or incident along the way often invite disaster by carrying so much weight that they travel more slowly and become more tired and thus more prone to the very accidents they were trying to guard against. The rule of thumb of not carrying more than 10% of one's personal body weight does not work if, like me, you are of very slight build. Indeed, my daughter, who is very slender, would barely be able to carry an empty rucksack if she stuck to that calculation! However, take as little as possible beyond the absolute essentials, not forgetting to include at least one luxury that will make the journey more enjoyable for you. This is a highly personal choice, ranging from Tabasco sauce to expensive soap or simply a favourite book, which can be read and reread.

The best way to discover the things you really need is to undertake some practice journeys. These will not only increase your fitness but will enable you to trial your rucksack, test your waterproofs and wear in your boots—the three most important and essential pieces of kit. Better to spend as much as possible on getting these right, and save on the extras, than risk the misery that ill-fitting boots or inadequate wet-weather gear will produce. There will always be a pilgrim who is better equipped than you are, or whose highly technical clothing you envy, but part of the challenge of the journey is in learning to live without even those things that you consider essential in daily life. Stripped of the part of our sense of self and status that depends on what we own, we can explore the nature of our real selves more easily. Divested of the disguise of our belongings, we can face the truth of our character when faced with difficulty and challenge, unprotected by the barrier of money and goods. Travelling lightly sets you free to the possibilities of adventure, of accepting the generosity of others gracefully and of discovering new and different ways of solving a problem, whether it is finding somewhere to stay, the best clothes to wear or the most effective blister remedy.

Ultimately, the most important thing to take with you on your journey is openness of heart and mind. Leave behind narrowness of vision and weight of expectation; such things will slow you down more than the heaviest of packs. Be prepared to be generous, to share your thoughts and feelings and to listen to those of others. Be ready to love, to laugh and to open your heart—to the landscape, the people and God.

Information for pilgrims

Traditionally, pilgrim routes were written up in books, which had the advantage that they could be carried along the route, but could not be changed or updated with any frequency. I have included the books I have used for each route, but access to the internet, with its wide-ranging and up-to-date information, is vital for pilgrimage planning.

Most of the walks described have dedicated websites, which are far and away the best place to begin when planning your pilgrimage. Information on routes, accommodation and transport to and from different locations will all be found on the websites below, as well as helpful suggestions about the type of terrain and highlights to visit.

Three main websites will give you access to general information on walking and pilgrimage as well as specific routes. The most significant one is for the Confraternity of St James (www.csj.org.uk), the organisation that holds information on many different routes and also provides the 'credencial', or pilgrim passport, for those wishing to gain a 'compostela' at the end of their journey to Santiago de Compostela.

Walkers in the UK do well to look first at the Long Distance Walkers Association site (www.ldwa.org.uk), which also offers general practical advice as well as being route-specific. It is particularly helpful in giving the Ordnance Survey map numbers for each route. Maps outside the UK can be ordered from specialist map sellers, but often the best place to get them is at the beginning of your route, from the local tourist office.

Walkopedia (www.walkopedia.net) is a good forum for exploration and exchange of information which might also prove useful.

In addition to these three, further route-specific information can be found in the following websites and books. This is not an exhaustive list and further searching will produce more information, but they are a good place to begin.

St Columba's Way: Iona to St Andrews

- This route has a dedicated website (www.thewayofstandrews.com) and also an entry on the LDWA site.

Via Ingles (Ferrol to Santiago de Compostela)

- The Confraternity of St James website (www.csj.org.uk) will provide all the information you need for this journey.
- Laura Perazzoli and Dave Whitson, *The Northern Caminos* (Cicerone, 2015)

Via Limovigensis (Vézelay to Limoges)

- The Confraternity of St James website (www.csj.org.uk) will provide all the information you need for this journey.
- The Dutch Association of St James produces an English version of its guidebook, obtainable here: www.gigaboek.nl/content/vezelayroute/boekinfo.htm. I used a French language version.

Pilgrim's Way (Winchester to Canterbury)

- Website: www.pilgrimswaycanterbury.org
- Sean Jennet, *The Pilgrims Way from Winchester to Canterbury* (Cassell, 1971)

St David's Way (Holywell to Bardsey Island)

- Website: www.pilgrims-way-north-wales.org. This is a useful website and kept up to date, although not all the signage was easily visible along the route.
- Carl Rogers and Tony Bowerman, *Wales Coast Path Llyn Peninsula* (Northern Eye, 2014)

Sentiero della Pace Francescano (Assisi to Gubbio)

- Information is harder to find in the UK, although the Club Alpino Italiano contains good instructions (www.caigubbio.it/francescano/francescano_ing.html). Better maps can be obtained in Assisi.
- Many websites offer a route description going the other way, towards Rome (www.agriturismolaquerciagentile.it/franciscan-trail-umbria.php)
- Trail guides are available in Italian and German.

The Jesus Trail (Tagbha to Capernaum)

- Website: www.jesustrail.com
- Anna Dinteman and David Landis, *Hiking the Jesus Trail* (Village to Village, 2013)

St James' Way (Worcester to Bristol)

- This is a complicated route but is mostly the Severn Way. It can be found as such on the LDWA website: www.ldwa.org.uk
- Terry Marsh, *The Severn Way* (Cicerone, 2014)

Thames Pilgrim's Way (Oxford to Binsey)

- The Thames Pilgrim's Way website offers a reflection for the section of the path that travels nearest to Binsey: www.thamespilgrimway. org.uk/stage-3.
- The most detailed information comes from the Thames Path guide on the National Trails website: www.nationaltrail.co.uk/thames-path
- More details still can be found in the Saturday Walkers Club circular walk description: www.walkingclub.org.uk/book_1/walk_13
- Leigh Hatts, *The Thames Path* (Cicerone, 2005)
- Ron Emmons, *Walks Along the Thames Path* (New Holland, 2008)

St Olav's Way (Stiklestad to Trondheim)

- The official website for this walk is very useful: www.pilegrimsleden. no/en/map/st.-olavs-leden
- Alison Raju, *Pilgrim Road to Nidaros* (Cicerone, 2001)

General information

- Long Distance Walkers Association, *The UK Trailwalkers Handbook* (Cicerone, 2009)
- John Pritchard, *Pocket Prayers for Pilgrims* (Church House Publishing, 2011)

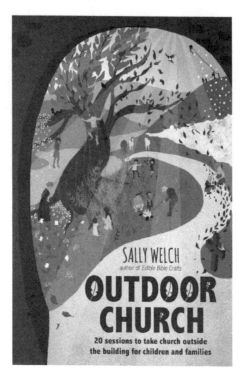

Helping churches to reconnect and value their environment, this is a creative worship and activity resource for churches to use outside the church building. *Outdoor Church* functions in any green space and is suitable for churches in urban, suburban and rural contexts. This book includes four sessions for each season and four stand-alone service outlines, based around the seasons. It also offers indoor alternatives for rainy days.

Outdoor Church
20 sessions to take church outside the building for children and families
Sally Welch

978 0 85746 416 3 £8.99

brfonline.org.uk

Celebrating
Festivals

Readings, reflections, crafts and prayer
activities for 20 major church festivals

Sally Welch

Ideal for use with all ages

Ideal for use in all-age worship, Sunday school, activity mornings or Messy Church events, this resource provides material for 20 major festivals throughout the church year. Each section has a unifying theme and includes a suggested Bible passages, a reflection for adults, a children's story and questions, a prayer activity, 'messy' craft activities and edible craft activities. An additional dimension links each festival to a part of the church building, helping children to understand the idea of sacred space and explore the relationship between the physical and the spiritual.

Celebrating Festivals
Readings, reflections, crafts and prayer activities
for 20 major church festivals
Sally Welch

978 0 84101 711 2 £8.99

brfonline.org.uk

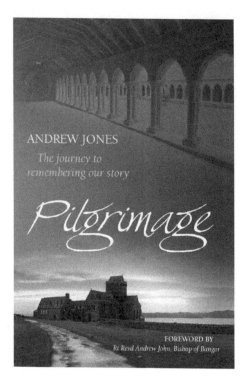

In this book, Andrew Jones shows how pilgrimage has the power to awaken those at all stages of belief to remembering the story of God's creating and redeeming work in history, the story that tells us who we are, where we have come from and where we are going. This not only offers a life-transforming way out of exile, but points to the way home, to the place where we can live an authentic and balanced life. The book concludes with a focus on eight popular places of pilgrimage in the British Isles, drawing out lessons from their history and spiritual heritage that can encourage and inspire us on our own faith journeys.

Pilgrimage
The journey to remembering our story
Andrew Jones

978 0 84101 834 8 £8.99

brfonline.org.uk

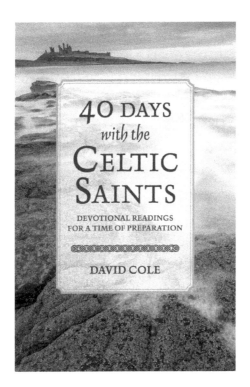

The life stories of the Celtic saints are inspirational. They demonstrate great and unassuming faith, often in the face of insurmountable difficulties. In *40 Days with the Celtic Saints*, David Cole draws us to relate our own life journey and developing relationship with God into the life story of the Celtic saint of the day. A corresponding biblical text and blessing encourages and motivates us to transform our lives for today's world in the light of such historic faith.

40 Days with the Celtic Saints
Devotional readings for a time of preparation
David Cole
978 0 85746 548 1 £7.99

brfonline.org.uk

BRF

Transforming
lives and communities

Christian growth and understanding of the Bible

Resourcing individuals, groups and leaders in churches for their own spiritual journey and for their ministry

Church outreach in the local community

Offering three programmes that churches are embracing to great effect as they seek to engage with their local communities and transform lives

Teaching Christianity in primary schools

Working with children and teachers to explore Christianity creatively and confidently

Children's and family ministry

Working with churches and families to explore Christianity creatively and bring the Bible alive

Visit **brf.org.uk** for more information on BRF's work
Review this book on Twitter using **#BRFconnect**

brf.org.uk

The Bible Reading Fellowship (BRF) is a Registered Charity (No. 233280)